Chestnuts, Galls, and Dandelion Wine

**Useful
Wild Plants
of the
Boston
Harbor Islands**

BOSTON HARBOR ISLANDS

North

Green Island

Little Calf Island

Outer Brewster

Calf Island

Middle Brewster

Great Brewster

Little Brewster

Deer Island

Lovell Island

Georges Island

Long Island

Gallops Island

Rainsford Island

Hog Island

HULL

Langlee Island

Sarah Island

Ragged Island

Castle Island

Spectacle Island

Thompson Island

Moon Island

Hangman Island

Peddocks Island

Sheep Island

Bumpkin Island

Nut Island

Grape Island

Slate Island

Raccoon Island

BOSTON

QUINCY

Chestnuts, Galls, and Dandelion Wine

Useful
Wild Plants
of the
Boston
Harbor Islands

William D. Perkins

THE PLANT PRESS, Halifax, Mass.
1982

Library of Congress Cataloging in Publication Data
Perkins, William D., 1924–
    Chestnuts, galls, and dandelion wine.

    Bibliography: p.
    Includes index.
    1. Plants, Useful—Massachusetts—Boston.
2. Boston Harbor Islands (Boston, Mass.)
I. Title.
QK98.4.U6P47   581.6'1'0974461   81-19867
ISBN 0-940960-00-1   AACR2

PRINTED IN THE UNITED STATES OF AMERICA

THE PLANT PRESS
P.O. BOX 133, HALIFAX, MA 02338-0133

FOR RUTH AND SUSAN

who haven't been there yet

ACKNOWLEDGEMENTS

Were it not for Dr. J. Towne Conover, who wrote the Foreword to this volume, my interest in the green world might never have gone beyond my stomach. The book, certainly, would never have been completed without his continual availability as mentor, sounding-board, and reader. Nor would the book have been completed without the help of others. In that way, it is no different than most books.

Had it not been for Jim Blake's permission to visit Thompson's Island on a regular basis, for example, I might never have seen the white chicory or developed a serious itch to visit the other islands. Had Elizabeth Lawrence, Faith Burbank, and others at the South Shore Natural Science Center not been willing to organize and participate in several summer field trips, and had the Quincy Party Boat Line been less flexible in routing and scheduling, fewer islands would have been so readily accessible. My thanks to all of them, to Ronald Clough (Senior Supervisor, Boston Harbor Islands), and to Gerald Flaherty (Wompatuck State Park Interpreter) for reading the manuscript, for their suggestions, and especially for the encouragement provided by their interest in this project.

Thanks are also due the many enthusiastic island managers who were knowledgeable and interested enough to point out some of the plants in unsuspected nooks and crannies, to Dot whose artistry with word-processor and camera had much to do with the final shape of the book and to Dover Publications, Inc., for permission to use selected illustrations by Regina O. Hughes from *Common Weeds of the United States*, their 1971 republication of *Selected Weeds of the United States* as originally published by the United States Department of Agriculture (Government Printing Office) in 1970.

AUTHOR'S NOTE:

Although the food and medicinal histories of plants in the book are repeatedly mentioned, it is not the author's purpose to promote those uses. Roots, crowns, young leaves, and blossoms of the dandelion, a plant seemingly known almost from birth by people of the northeast, are well known as ingredients in herbal medicines and a great variety of foods and beverages. The plants are grown commercially in Maine and New Jersey and can be found on the shelves with gourmet foods in some supermarkets.

But there are many other plants used as food and medicine which are less familiar and more difficult to identify. Among them are some in which certain parts are always poisonous or which may become poisonous during certain stages in their development. Some are only mildly toxic. A few are deadly. Cooking sometimes destroys principles which make certain plants poisonous in the raw state. Other poisonous principles are not destroyed by cooking. A

[6]

particular species of plant grown in one field may be eaten with no harmful effects while the same species grown in another field may be unsafe to use as food. Differences in individual human beings make some plants which are harmless for one dangerous for another. The point here is not to elaborate on these considerations, but to emphasize that to use wild plants safely as either food or medicine requires skills and knowledge developed only by study and experience. Use of the plants as food or medicine by persons not thoroughly familiar with them, and with *all* risks and cautions governing that use, is emphatically discouraged.

Besides, the book is designed to assist and encourage "looking" rather than "grazing" or "collecting." Do your collecting in mainland fields. Leave plants on the islands as undisturbed as possible. It would not take long, with the thousands of visitors the islands receive each year, for the collecting urge to seriously deplete some species. Though they may often appear firmly established, the tenure of some island plants is hazardous at best.

With that, let me close this note with an admonition from a woman of the old sod, mother of a lawyer friend:

> "Never give us cause to say, 'for shame, these
> places were more beautiful before you came.'"

William D. Perkins

CONTENTS

PART ONE

WHERE FROM AND WHAT FOR

. . . for magic

. . . for telling fortunes

. . . to drive away vermin

. . . to keep things clean and smelling nice

. . . for color

. . . for toys and games

. . . for whistles, flutes, and sambukes

. . . for healing

A more detailed look at ways in which each of twenty-five selected wild plants has been used. Plants are arranged in groups according to blossom color.

PART TWO

FIELD GUIDE

Illustrations, descriptions, more discussion, and island locations for each of the twenty-five selected plants. Plants arranged in groups according to blossom color.

FOREWORD

When I received the manuscript of *Chestnuts, Galls, and Dandelion Wine,* I was unprepared for what Bill Perkins put into my hands. It had some very unusual qualities for a park guide-book. I had the distinct feeling that Bill was trying to tell us something about opposing forces in nature. Good and evil, pictured as the struggle of opposites, characterized by anger and violence pitted against peace and freedom, were observed to be playing a historical role out on the Boston Harbor Islands. What a dramatic way to introduce the reader to this imaginative book.

I gather Bill wants us, as visitors, to have a total experience on these historic islands. This is not just another guide to the wildflowers of a historical site. It is far more. Bill wants us to include a recognition of the lowly weeds underfoot for what they are and, in turn, to hear what they are trying to tell us about the past, the present, and the future of human beings. The writer makes this quite clear when he gives us examples of *Achillea* (yarrow), *Polygonum* (Lady's thumb), and *Pinus* (pine tree) and how these plants were related to peoples down through the millennia. This account is a perspective of history through a study of some wild plants that have been linked in some fascinating ways with man's own struggle for survival.

You may remember that human beings and plants have evolved together. Oh yes, human beings are late comers, but during those brief millions of years of human evolution from prehominid to *Homo sapien* there has been a mutually dependent pact between humans and plants. *Homo* has depended upon plants for food and medicines, while plants have depended upon *Homo* for distribution and survival. This insight, for me, makes a trip to the harbor islands all the more exciting and meaningful because I can witness the unfolding of the past, not only through park plaques and brochures, but by way of actually seeing the relics of man's past violence . . . . the buildings, the fortifications, the prison cells, the outlook across the harbor as despair-filled eyes must once have seen it.

Then, amid all these relics of man's occupation, there are the weeds. They grow in the chinks of the ruins and border the pathways. They scrabble for perches, getting rootholds on the edges of walls. Plants fight drifting sands along the beaches above the storm berms, always defying the poisoning effects of salt air just to exist. This tenacity is very like that of the people who were held prisoner here, or who, in struggling to leave one hopeless life in the Old World, exchanged it for another full of unknowns and fears. Often these people, like the hermit of Green Island, hung on and survived almost insurmountable difficulties. The weeds on the islands demonstrate daily this continuing struggle for survival shared by man and plant over millions of years.

We are fortunate to have brought together for us such a rich history of peoples, folklore, superstition, and the role of plants (lowly weeds, if you will) through ancient times and yesteryears. There is good reason why Bill has the diversity of background to write such a lively and interesting account. Many of his professional years were spent as an educator and administrator in public schools. Most of his intellectual life, though, lay outside the classroom walls. He was constantly looking for a simpler way of living and desired a more reflective existence than the hectic pace of today's school administrator. I don't think Bill ever fully accepted the effects and choices thrust on society by the Industrial Revolution. He lives today, with his cultivated weed garden, in a self-chosen rural setting in southeastern Massachusetts, off the beaten track and away from the trafficking of the commercial world. There he devotes his hours to a study of wild plants, colonial archaeology, and the writing of books about his favorite subjects; plants and human beings.

Somewhat late in life Bill stumbled upon plants as an outlet for his consuming curiosity. Mostly, he is self-taught and today has become a fine, respected amateur botanist and the local authority on edible wild plants. He is on the staff of the South Shore Natural Science Center in Norwell, Massachusetts. This blend of historian-educator-writer-botanist has brought out those qualities which you, the reader, will enjoy in this unusual account of plants and humans.

The first section of the book provides a background for those less familiar with the curious tales and uses of the plants as well as something of the origins of their names. If you are luke-warm about the subject at the outset, you may well be keenly interested in these plant stories by the time you finish reading this section. What follows is a set of stories spun around twenty-five of the most common ubiquitous weeds in the Old and New Worlds alike, weeds that we have underfoot everywhere. Their very commonness has relegated them to ignominy and neglect. At best, most weeds are thought of as pests, nuisances to be rid of.

Bill gives us a new and impressive look at these weeds in a historical context. He opens up myriads of windows into the past lives of human beings in cultures all over the world. Each plant species brings forth a fascinating series of anecdotes, folktales, and plant uses we may not have dreamed possible. The common names of plants take on new meaning from events in the lives of peoples long dead. It is even possible that you, the reader, may decide to explore the literature of this subject further. It is fascinating, I can assure you.

But now, do take the time to read the book. Once you have done so, a trip to the islands will take on a whole new dimension. In fact, I doubt that any island will ever be the same for you.

J. Towne Conover

INTRODUCTION

Horse chestnuts, oak galls, and dandelions are all to be found on the Boston Harbor Islands — chestnuts to ease the ache in aging bones, galls to foretell the future, and dandelions to make a sparkling wine that will carry summer right through the winter.

But chestnuts, galls, and dandelion wine are not apt to come quickly to mind when one first visits the islands. From what attracts the eye and from much of what there is to read about island history, the idea that theirs is a story of violence and hardship is more likely to occur. The record is fat with tales of fort and prison, quarantine and almshouse, shipwreck and drowning, murder, trial, hanging, and burial. All else seems slim by comparison. Featured items for many of the islands are ramparts, gun emplacements, and dank underground rooms and corridors. Without question, they are reminders of violence and hardship, clenched fists guarding the harbor entrance.

As with most symbols, though, the meaning is complex and two-sided. Designed for violence, to create hardship or to relieve it, the fortifications, the prisons, the almshouses, the quarantine stations are reminders that those who were here before us found it necessary to protect the things they held dear, just as we do today.... things like human dignity, freedom, brotherhood, and the rights of individuals. Incongruous as the idea might seem, they were created as acts of love. And that should be as much a part of their record as the violence.

Island wild plants and their flowers, on the other hand, are so familiar that they seem to go unnoticed even when they are underfoot. They show up only occasionally in accounts of island history and, more often than not, no thought of violence is associated with them. They are seen simply as pesky weeds or, once in awhile, as beautiful wild blossoms seeming to signal what peaceful places the islands have become. Almost invariably they stimulate thoughts of love and peace. But violence and hardship are a part of their story just as love and peace belong to the story of fort and prison.

Yarrow's generic name is *Achillea* because it was supposed to have been used by Achilles to stop the bleeding of his soldiers' wounds during the Trojan War. So used it was an instrument of mercy, but in the language of flowers "yarrow" means "war."

A little knotweed known as Lady's thumb is scattered over the islands. It is a harmless plant and yet it has served the superstition-ridden black arts as an agent for the slow and painful elimination of unwanted neighbors.

Pine trees have been used as famine food by American Indians. They stripped great quantities of the inner bark from large areas of trees, dried it, and set it aside as insurance against hard times of winter. The name *Adirondack* means "tree-eaters."

It does no harm to be reminded that violence and hardship have been pervasive parts of the island story. It helps fix in the mind how persistent some aspects of history can be. How little changed, for example, are the basics of relationships among human beings. We defend and we aggress. It has always been so. In between the visible violence we tend the land, raise our families, question our world and cock curious eyes at others. All the while the good and the bad continue side by side.

Nothing illustrates this better than stories of the plants found growing wild on the islands today. Theirs, too, is a record of the worst as well as the best in human history. It extends far into the past, long pre-dating the comparatively short sojourn for many of them on the islands. It is a record of the humorous, the religious, the superstitious, the trivial, the magic, and the tragic. The stories which make it up are artifacts of an imperishable human curiosity, imagination, and ingenuity.

The knowledge that almost every wild plant carries stories which seem to be limitless in number and variety may come as a surprise. But the more we look into them, the better we understand just how long the plants have been around, how closely they have been tied to human activity, and how freely many of them have spread to places other than their home countries. The process has been accidental at times, deliberate at other times. Seeds of plantain, for example, which were unintentionally carried around in the clothing and possessions of early settlers, fell to the ground and took root wherever the settlers moved. Growth of plants not present in their territory before the white-men arrived did not pass unnoticed by the Indians and they named the plantain "white-man's foot." Seeds of bouncing Bet, on the other hand, were brought to this country and cultivated intentionally so that the plant would be available for use as soap and medicine.

In both cases the plants had long histories of use by people in other parts of the world and each had already acquired a good assortment of stories. In both cases the plants spread on their own once they had arrived, continued to be used, and continued to add new tales to their individual stores of folklore.

Unless the island visitor is a wild-food enthusiast, or a student of botany and folklore, he may never realize that the wild plants growing there have been a great deal more than incidental and bothersome companions. Or, if it *is* known that the plants have played important parts in man's journey through time, the fact that much of the information is not in the mainstream, is scattered through specialized books and periodicals requiring a special interest and directed effort to collect, may serve to keep the stories out of reach.

For most of us it is the information at our fingertips or the things we discover for ourselves which are most likely to capture and hold attention. How easy it is to recall past pleasures when the reminders are all in one place. When I read about chicory on page 97, the sight of a plant bearing blossoms whiter even than daisy petals always comes to mind. Before its discovery all of the chicory blossoms I had ever seen, in fields and along roadsides and railroad tracks, had been blue. It is what I had learned to expect, and to come suddenly on an exception snuggled into a corner outside the gym on Thompson's Island proved a memorable experience indeed.

Reading about shepherd's purse, I am reminded of the unexpected discovery of one of its cousins on an isolated island beach. Having a special interest in crucifers, I recognized dittander *(Lepidium latifolium)* as a member of the mustard family as soon as I found it, but it was clearly a species I had not seen before. When I finally confirmed its identity with the Concord Field Station of Harvard's Museum of Comparative Zoology and with the University of Massachusetts at Amherst, the curators of each asked for herbarium specimens and I experienced another of those special pleasures, the likes of which have the power to enrich our lives.

For me, there is a certain compatability between those pleasures and the thumbing of a book by a warm fire on a cold winter night. So it is as much for myself, as for anyone else, that I have arranged, set down, and bound this collection of assorted stories about some of the wild plants which have attracted my attention. They are my own special reminders about trips to those special places . . . . the islands of Boston Harbor.

PART I

WHERE FROM AND WHAT FOR

It has already been mentioned that not all of the plants found growing wild on the islands are from this part of the world. Many of them were brought here from faraway places. Some arrived accidentally while others were brought intentionally for food and other purposes. Asparagus, whose feathery fronds can be seen forcing a way through the poison ivy on the North-facing banks of Gallops Island in late summer, was brought to this country as a food by early settlers, but no one knows, for certain, how or when it arrived on the island.

Perhaps Peter Newcomb included it among the vegetables to be grown on the farm he had there in the early 1800's. Maybe his wife, Margaret, kept it to grow in her kitchen garden and it stayed on to play a part in the reputation enjoyed by the cooking at the eating establishment she opened there after Peter died. Once the inn closed its doors and the old farm was deserted, the asparagus may have wandered off, found the banks more to its liking than the garden, and so put down its roots.

Though it has earned a reputation as a wanderer in its own right, asparagus has been carried far and wide by men who valued it for food, for medicine, and for its supposed ability to excite passion. There was a time when kings and wealthy persons of Europe attempted to monopolize asparagus by placing it under guard in their private gardens and making it unlawful for others to grow or possess it. Not surprisingly, such efforts proved to be exercises in futility and served only to encourage bribery and theft by those outside the privileged ranks who could obtain the plant in no other way.

As far as its presence on Gallops Island is concerned, some of the seeds may have been included in ballast dumped on the beach from an unknown ship. At one time the ballast heaps at every major port along the East coast were hunting spots favored by botanists because new plants often appeared there. Then, of course, there is always the possibility that asparagus was simply dropped on the island as a seed which had run its course through a passing bird.

No matter how asparagus, or any of the other "green immigrants," arrived on the islands, stories have come along with them and knowing even a little about them can add pleasure to a day on the islands. The sight of chicory's blue flowers in an island field assumes a special significance, for example, when it is known that Governor Bowdoin brought some of the plants from Holland in 1785 and planted them around his house in Dorchester with the intention of using them as greens. In its report of 1896, the United States Department of Agriculture said that the chicory spread from the yard to all waste ground in the vicinity. Looking back from the islands, across the water toward Dorchester's hills, it is easy to imagine that chicory which now grows on the islands came originally from Holland by way of the Governor's front yard.

Among the plants which surround the visitor to the islands are many which have been used for things other than food.

There are Plants of Magic

Part of chicory's story is one of mystery and magic. Its possession was believed to give one the power to open mountains and gain access to the great treasures which were supposed to have been hidden inside of them. More fitting for the thoughts of those imprisoned in island forts over the years, though, might have been the belief that a chicory plant cut from the ground on July 25th would make its bearer invisible and, at the same time, could be used to open doors secured by the strongest locks. Desperate hopes for freedom might have been enough to dismiss as trivial all thoughts of chicory's long, tough roots and the condition that for the magic to work the plant had to be dug in absolute silence at midnight with a knife of pure gold.

Beliefs connected with some of the plants encouraged the mind to work its own magic. The galls of goldenrod were thought to be good for preventing rheumatism and arthritis. Unlike familiar medicines which were to be taken internally or applied externally, the galls had only to be carried about in a pocket. If pains happened to appear, it was taken only as a sign that the grub inside the gall was no longer alive, not that the magic had failed. In such cases the sufferer would have to seek out another gall with a living grub inside it. Horse chestnuts, to which the same virtues were assigned, had an advantage over the galls in that there was no grub to worry about. They were good as long as they lasted.

There are Fortune-Tellers Among Them

Some island plants are monuments to those indomitable souls dedicated to finding ways to pierce the screen which hides tomorrow's fortunes. Their stories are tributes to imagination and ingenuity, if not to credibility. And it is interesting to note that even though the majority of fortunes to be read from a particular plant may be bad, there is always at least one good one to keep the hopeful coming back. It was once considered hazardous to dream of walking through a blackberry patch, for example. If one were pricked in the dream, it meant that a good friend would do you harm. To have the thorns draw blood signalled more bad luck in that it was supposed to foretell serious problems in business. But there was always the chance of good omens for if one were fortunate enough to walk through the blackberry patch neither pricked nor bloodied, triumph over enemies was assured. Those yearning for a chance to give the belief a modern test will find bramble patches enough on the islands to assure haunted dreams.

Whenever there are oak trees, and the islands have their share, there will be galls. These too have caught the eyes of soothsayers over the years, though predictions made with their help were less personal than those of the brambles.

At different times in its development, the occupant of a particular gall will appear as a grub or as a fly-like wasp. For anyone who cut open a gall with the intention of predicting the future on the basis of what was found inside, two possibilities were present early in the game. Once the gall's original occupant had completed its development and bored its way to freedom, the exit opening made the shelter available for passing spiders and exploring ants and the possibilities were thereby raised to four. Each held a different meaning for the true believer. To discover a grub was understood to mean that much disease lay ahead for cattle and other farm animals. To find the tiny wasp meant war. A spider meant there would be sickness and death among men. To find an ant was the single encouraging discovery for it meant that the coming year would be a good one for grain.

There are Plants to Drive Away Vermin

In the old days moths, mosquitoes, flies, fleas, rats, mice, and snakes were no more welcome than they are today and imaginations were always at work trying to find new ways to keep them under control. Fragrant fern-like leaves of tansy appear very early in the spring on the islands. They develop bitter-button blossoms late in the summer and persist far into fall. The first plants were brought to New England by early settlers and planted in gardens as kitchen and medicinal herbs. Tansy was also pressed into service as a plant whose leaves, if rubbed into fresh meat would keep it free of flies and, if strewn around the floor, would do a good job of keeping them out of the house as well. Present day island visitors sometimes rub the leaves on their faces, arms, and necks to keep away mosquitoes.

Catnip, a member of the mint family, is best known as a cat intoxicant, but it has also been used to ease the stings of bees and wasps and to drive away rats. If there is any truth to its reported rat-repelling powers, it must not have been growing on Spectacle Island in 1934, for Edward Rowe Snow wrote that the rats there at that time were plentiful, bold, and large as cats.

Other island plants have been used in the same ways as tansy and catnip. Mayweed has been used to keep away flies and fleas. Mullein has been used against mice, yarrow against ants, and butter and eggs to poison flies.

There are Plants to keep things Clean and Smelling Nice

Keeping things clean and smelling nice was not always as easy as it is today. And there are those who will say that it isn't so easy today either. It must be admitted, though, that it's probably a lot easier now than it was when those things which served as forerunners to modern soaps, detergents, deodorants, and air-fresheners had to be made completely from natural materials gathered in nearby woods and fields.

Horsetails were sought as scouring pads. They were used to clean metal gun parts and to scour pewter. The old names "gunbright" and "scouring rush" suggest the uses. Bruised leaves of bouncing Bet, also known as soapwort, scourwort, and latherwort were used by the Pilgrims to clean woodenware and pewter. The plant is still valued as particularly helpful in cleaning delicate old fabrics. The ashes of burned ferns, stalks and blossoms of sweet-pepper bush, and crushed roots of lambsquarters were all once used as emergency soap material.

Strewing herbs, like tansy, not only helped to drive away flies and fleas, but the pleasant fragrance they emitted when walked over helped to keep the house smelling good. Dried flowers and leaves of sweet clover, when put into drawers with linen, kept it smelling nice and when used with furs acted like a camphor in keeping moths away. Mugwort is said to have done the same for woolen clothing, and chips of red cedar have long been known for the protection and fragrance they give to bureau drawers and to closets.

There are Plants to use for Color

Before the development of chemical dyes colors for yarn and cloth were obtained from plants. The despised ragweed was used to make a green dye. Violet came from elderberry, red from barberry, yellow from goldenrod, black from sumac, and tan from poke. By experimenting with different parts of many plants, and by using different mordanting agents, early settlers had a wide range of color available to them.

Not only were the plant dyes used to color finished cloth and yarns, they were also used to color hair. A wash of blackberry leaves boiled in lye was used to make hair black. The women of Rome were said to have used an infusion of mullein flowers to dye their hair a golden color and a soap made from the ashes of the burned plant was believed to restore gray hair to its original color.

A red writing ink was obtained from pokeberry, a brown ink from oak galls, and the sap of poison ivy provided an indelible black used for marking laundry. Juice from the pokeberries was also used to color cake frostings and wine, but the practice was discontinued because of uncertainty about the poisonous qualities of the berries and because wine drinkers said the juice ruined the flavor of their wine.

The fact that velvety mullein would produce a rouge-like glow when rubbed against a cheek was not missed by country girls and they used the leaves for that purpose when make-up was prohibited. A species of Lady's thumb yielded to Chinese imagination in the belief that if a root from a fifty-year old plant were taken internally every day for one year it would insure the preservation of black hair and beard.

There are Plants for Toys and Games

Every once in a while the name "two-heads-entangled" is used for violets. It is the translation of an Onandaga Indian name for a game their children played with the blossoms. To play, each of two children took a violet. The flower heads were interlocked and then pulled apart by the stem. The child whose blossom survived the pull was the winner. There are similar undertones of violence in a game known as "kemps", from the Old English *cempa* which means "warrior." It is played with plantain flower stalks by children in England and Scotland. Two children collect an equal number of stalks and then take turns trying to knock the heads from one "warrior" at a time. The child with the last flower stalk which has the head still attached is the winner. American children use dandelion stems and blossoms in the same way. When a blossom is struck off, the successful striker shouts "ha, ha, I knocked the baby's head off." Some children use thumbs to snap the blossoms from the stems and, when successful, chant "mother had a baby and the head fell off."

At one time country boys would chase one another with nettle whips or throw burdock burrs into little girls' curls for a change of pace. The burrs are now more apt to be thrown at felt bulls'-eyes, as a safe form of darts, or collected and used as Tinker Toys and Erector Sets by taking advantage of the ease with which they cling to one another and just about anything else they touch.

The dried stems of cattails make fine toy logs and the fluff of both cattails and milkweed has been used to stuff dolls and toy animals.

There are Plants for Whistles, Flutes, and Sambukes

The elderberry bush is sometimes called the "boortree", a name more properly assigned to its larger and woodier European relative. But the name is said to come from the ease with which the pith can be pushed (bored) from the center of old stems when they are to be made into the familiar whistles and flutes. So it is really not an inappropriate name for our elderberry bush. But anyone wishing to tackle a mystery of names may want to try tracking down *the* reason for the generic name *Sambucus*. There are at least two explanations and both center around musical instruments supposed to have been made from elderwood. One instrument, the sambuke, is a harp-like stringed instrument while the other, the sackbut, is a wind instrument which was the forerunner to the trombone. The correct interpretation stands presently as a coin-toss with the coin still in the air.

Whistles made from acorn caps and willow stems are familiar things. The willow whistles are usually spring projects for boys and their grandfathers, but most grandfathers soon learn to steer clear of the little squeaker that gave dandelion the name of "bumpipe." It's a bum pipe alright, and hard enough to get tooting, but it does make a noise like an anemic Bronx cheer and it *is* liked by some boys. Basically, it is nothing more than a two-inch piece of dandelion stem which is mashed at one end with the teeth until it flattens out into something like an oboe reed and squeals when blown through. It's good anytime of year just so long as you can find a dandelion stem, have the patience to make it squeal, and can stand the bitter taste which gave the plant the name Devil's milkpail.

There are Plants for Healing

It is almost impossible to think of a single human ailment which has not, at one time or another, been treated with a lotion or potion made from a wild plant. The problems have included those which affect large groups of people as well as the more familiar ones which we individually scratch, dab, and dose every day. The list covers external as well as internal problems .... rashes, abrasions, wounds, dandruff, nervousness, headache, worms, stomach distress, kidney ailments, liver complaints, and many more.

Charles F. Millspaugh, writer about American medicinal plants, tells us that the ailanthus tree, introduced to this country about 1800 as an ornamental, was also valued because it was believed to absorb malarial poisons from the air. The occurrence of epidemics in several of our larger cities after its introduction, however, almost led to its extermination. It seems that some people, seeking causes for the epidemics, decided that the ailanthus smelled so bad during its flowering period because it was releasing all of the noxious gasses it had absorbed and stored during the rest of the year. They felt that the trees should be destroyed and set out to do what they could about it. Bad feelings eventually disappeared, though, the trees survived and today grow like weeds all over Boston and on the harbor islands.

Many wild plants served more than one medicinal purpose. While some people carried around bits of plantain root as insurance against being bitten by snakes, for example, others saved the leaves which made good poultices and were believed effective in drawing out poison from the bites of spiders and other insects. If not needed as poultices, they could always be used for tea to relieve certain bowel problems or used to tell whether it was time to take the hay into the barn.

Skin abrasions could be treated with a lotion made from tansy leaves soaked nine days in buttermilk and, in spite of some reputation as a poisonous plant, tansy was sometimes used to make a tea for calming jumpy nerves, though it was more often suggested that its durable golden blossoms be included in winter bouquets for that purpose.

Juice from crushed jewelweed was sometimes rubbed on foreheads to relieve headaches or used as a skin wash to prevent poison ivy. "Summer complaint," better known as diarrhea, was occasionally treated with a tea made from Mayweed. The hot tea could also be used as a wash to relieve rheumatic pains.

Not only has it been necessary for people to have the means to treat illness and to care for injuries suffered from attack or accident but, as we have seen, there have been other needs to satisfy, many of them identical with those which must be satisfied today. They felt it necessary to know what the future held, to have some magic for controlling destiny, to play, to make music, to keep themselves and their possessions attractive in all ways. What could have been more natural, in earlier and less developed times, than for people to turn to the plants around them for assistance in such things?

As we begin to accumulate specific information about individual plants, the resourcefulness of our ancestors in putting them to use becomes increasingly impressive.

AMARANTH
Amaranthus retroflexus L.

The name "amaranth" came originally from *amarantos*, a Greek word for "unfading" or "unwithering," but over the years confusions as to endings and spellings changed its original form and it comes to us as *amor-anthus*, "love-flower" or "flower-of-love." Because of its long-lasting qualities, the Greeks are supposed to have believed the plant was immortal and, as a result, it became a plant of mystery cults, a decorator of religious statues and tombs, and gave its name to a Swedish order of knighthood known as "Amaranter."

There are many species of amaranth and they differ so greatly in appearance that some people say the more attractive ones are called amaranths and the weedy, less attractive, ones are known as pigweeds. Another version says that the name "pigweed" refers to a love pigs seem to have for the plant as food.

Amaranth has also served well as a human food. One species, *Amaranthus hypochondriacus*, is presently undergoing testing as a grain crop. The species found growing wild on the Boston Harbor Islands, *Amaranthus retroflexus*, is more often used as a spinach plant, though Indians in Arizona and southwestern Colorado have used the ground seeds for mush, gruel, and bread. The book *Amaranth*, by John N. Cole, is one of the best sources of information about the plant.

Since a single plant may produce as many as 196,405 seeds, and since it seems to grow wild so easily and well, it is not hard to understand why it is so common or why it might be called "careless weed."

We are sometimes told that a high saponin content in the leaves has encouraged the use of amaranth to wash clothes. Medicinally, the plant is reported to have been used to stop internal bleeding, diarrhea, and excessive menstrual flow.

CATTAIL
Typha latifolia L.

A survey made by the Federal Government during World War II showed that if all the seeds of the cattails from the 140,000 square miles of cattail-producing swamp in the United States were processed, the result would be 34,000,000 pounds of oil and 166,000,000 pounds of meal for cattle and chicken feed.

Shortly after the war, workers from the Cattail Research Center at Syracuse University found that the roots from only one acre of cattails would yield approximately 32 tons of flour.

At the same time they pointed to some other possibilities for cattails. They found, for example, that ethyl-alcohol for anti-freeze can be produced from the fermented flour of the roots, that fibers of the plant can be used to stuff furniture and to make burlap and webbing, that an adhesive can be made from the stems, and that the flowers can be made into an efficient insulating material.

But long before cattails attracted the attention of government and university researchers, they caught the eyes and imaginations of others. A cattail was supposed to have been put into the hand of Jesus as a mock sceptre during the crowning with thorns. The name "reed-mace" comes from that idea.

Juices of the plant provided a candy for Indian children and, from the roots, their elders extracted a sweetening syrup for their puddings. Starchy material from the roots and pollen from the flowers make the plant a double-ended producer of flours which can be used to thicken soups and to make tasty breads.

The down has been used as padding for quilts, pillows, vests, toys, and Indian cradle-boards. Mountain men have stuffed it into their boots to prevent frost-bite and, at the other extreme, it has been mixed with swine's grease and used to heal burns from fire and scalding from water.

CURLY DOCK
Rumex crispus L.

The old belief that useful plants carried signs in their color, form, smell, taste, or feel to indicate what purposes they were created to serve is known as the Doctrine of Signatures. Examples of such signs at work are to be seen in the section on Lady's thumb. Similar examples can be found for almost every useful plant, particularly those with real or imagined medicinal powers.

Every once in a while you might be surprised by stirrings of the doctrine within yourself. Try to pull curly dock out by the roots, for example. You might get the idea that it is a lot like pulling teeth. If so, you are right on target and it probably won't surprise you to learn that some of the old medicinal remedies which included dock had to do with teeth. The leaves, used as greens, were believed to tighten loose teeth. An infusion of the roots in wine was supposed to relieve toothache and the dried and ground roots were supposed to provide a good toothpowder.

In addition to their use as tooth-tighteners, dock leaves are sometimes used, even now, as a remedy for stinging caused by nettles. Explanations are usually accompanied by a charm-verse which, we are told, is to be recited as the injured area is rubbed with the crushed leaves.

"Nettle in, dock out,
Dock in, nettle out;
Nettle in, dock out,
Dock rub nettle out."

Having ignored the verse in haste to relieve the irritating sting, some will swear that the remedy is effective, verse or no verse.

LAMBSQUARTERS
Chenopodium album L.

The Chinese used lambsquarters to heal burns and to relieve the itching of insect bites. It has been used as a mild laxative and Indians made a tea of it to relieve stomach pains. But by far the greatest use of lambsquarters has been as food. There are few plants better suited to illustrate the long and close relationship between man and some of the plants he now ignores or goes to great lengths to avoid, destroy or eliminate.

Fossils indicate that lambsquarters was growing in England and was part of the human diet during the Neolithic, Bronze, and Early Iron Ages. The Romans ate lambsquarters regularly. Remnants of the plant have been found in early lake villages of Switzerland, it was eaten as greens in the Hebrides Islands off the west coast of Scotland and, in our own country, has been collected and used by the Navajos, Pueblos, Diggers, and Utahs. The plant is found in North America, the British Isles, continental Europe, Africa, Asia, and Australia.

In 1950 a body recovered from a peat bog in Denmark, where it had been for 2000 years, was so well preserved that botanists and archaeologists were able to determine the contents of the man's last meal. It had consisted of a gruel which contained, among other things, lambsquarters, black bindweed, and persicaria, all of which grow as weeds on the Boston Harbor Islands today.

When cultivated spinach came along weeds such as lambsquarters fell out of favor. When they are compared for food value and flavor it is hard to understand why the weeds were ever dropped. In the simple comparison below, food values are for 100 grams uncooked.

	Calories	Protein	Carbohydrates	Fiber	Calcium	Iron	Vitamin C	Vitamin A
Spinach	26	3.2	4.3	.6	93	3.1	21	8,100
Lambsquarters	43	4.2	7.3	2.1	309	1.2	80	11,600
Amaranth	36	3.5	6.5	1.3	267	3.9	80	6,100
	grams	grams	mg	mg	mg	mg		I.U.

MUGWORT
Artemisia vulgaris L.

Before the introduction of hops, mugwort was used to flavor beer and some people believe that is where the name comes from. Since one definition of the word "wort" says that it is a liquid prepared with malt which, after fermenting, becomes beer, it can be said that we derive from this plant a beverage for steins, a "wort" of the "mug" so to speak. But another definition of "wort" tells us that it is a plant, an herb, or a vegetable. And there are those people who believe that it is in this sense we must interpret the name. Mug, they say, does not refer to a container for beer any more than "wort" refers to a beverage. The name comes to us from an Anglo-Saxon word, *mucgwyrt*, which is a plant *(wyrt)* useful against such things as gnats, flies, and biting midges *(mucg?)*.

As to mugwort being a plant of superstition, though, there is no doubt. It will be seen that yarrow and burdock are said to provide us with a means to satisfy questions of the heart. Here we learn that to sleep on a pillow of mugwort is to court dreams of one's entire future.

A sprig of mugwort under a doormat is supposed to keep away annoying persons. A sprig hung over the door, if the stories are to be believed, will protect against lightning. If the mugwort be collected on St. John's Eve (June 23) there will be added protection against disease. If it is worn as a crown on that same evening, the wearer will be protected against all evil.

But the island visitor, weary with too much walking and needing protection from too much sun, might be mugwort's greatest fan for, if it is placed in the shoes, mugwort is supposed to protect against fatigue, sunstroke, *and* wild beasties.

POISON IVY
Rhus radicans L.

As a useful plant, poison ivy serves as an example that a plant need not be eaten to be toxic. Nettle is another familiar one, but poison ivy's defense is so refined that its effect may be produced without direct contact with the plant. The irritating oil may be carried on the fur of animals, on the varnished surface of a croquet ball, or may even ride a wisp of smoke across space to strike an unsuspecting passer-by. Delayed appearance of rash and blisters increases the chance that the plant's location will pass unnoticed, or be forgotten, and so decrease the likelihood anyone will return to destroy it. Such a finesse for survival could be no more effective were it a deliberate act.

The number of different antidotes which are suggested attests to poison ivy's ability to stimulate human ingenuity. Jewelweed, plantain, sweetfern, elderberry, butter and eggs, ragweed, bouncing-bet, and onions are among the plants of the eastern United States which are said to be useful in treating or preventing poisoning from poison ivy. Other suggested means have included unleaded gasoline, Fels-naptha-soap (not bath soap), baking soda, Epsom salts, boric acid compresses, and — perhaps best of all — a visit to the doctor.

As to other uses, poison ivy has served as a diuretic, a treatment for ringworm and other skin disorders, as a dye, an indelible laundry marker, and as an ingredient for varnishes used to finish boots and shoes.

But the best use of all is as a lesson in plant identification. Learn to recognize it and then *LET POISON IVY ALONE.*

BUTTER AND EGGS
Linaria vulgaris Mill.

An interesting thing about many of the wild plants found on the islands and elsewhere, is how they so often seem plagued by resemblance. Before butter and eggs blossoms, for example, it resembles flax, so one of its common names has become flaxweed and its generic name, *Linaria*, comes from the Latin *linum*, which means "flax."

Careful examination of a blossom will reveal a resemblance to the mouth of a toad and putting that resemblance together with a resemblance to flax provides at least one explanation of the name "toadflax."

Since the blossoms have a strong family resemblance to true snapdragons, the plant is also known as "snapdragon." The colors, resembling yellow butter and orange egg-yolks, seem to have been enough reason to have given it the name "butter and eggs," though it is never mentioned as an edible plant, and those who have risked tasting it have reacted to the acrid juices by calling it "gallwort."

For those who are not sure of a plant's identity, tasting is always a *real* risk. For example: without the blossoms there is a strong resemblance between this plant and a toxic spurge known as *Esula* or wolf's milk. The similarities are so great that someone, when wild plants were more commonly used as food and medicine, prepared a verse so that others might not fall victim to the plague of resemblance and the possibly painful aftereffects of mistaking one plant for the other. Using the blistering milky sap which flows from a broken piece of spurge as a distinguishing feature, the rhyme goes:

> "Esula with milke doth flow,
> Toadflax without milke doth grow."

But with all of these resemblances and the names they have produced, the most frequently noted use for butter and eggs seems to have produced no name at all. It has been said that the plant, scalded in milk and placed in little bowls about the house, is an effective fly-poison.

DANDELION
Taraxacum officinale Weber

At Upsala, in Sweden, dandelions open their blossoms about five in the morning and close them between eight and ten a.m. In Innsbruck, Austria, the times range between six in the morning and three in the afternoon and, in our part of the world, they open about four a.m. and close between twelve and two p.m. on sunny days.

None of this seems of much importance except to persons who, like the Swedish botanist Linnaeus, wish to plant time-telling gardens. In that case, it is nice to know at approximately what time the blossoms can be expected to open and close so that a proper place can be reserved for them in the floral clock.

To fill a belly and dispel a thirst are more familiar uses of dandelions. For centuries the greens have been gathered as a spring tonic or simply as good potherb and salad material. Directions are to be found for much more than boiling greens and tossing salads, though. There are also those for wine, shrub, beer, tea, coffee, cordial, omelet, bread, jello, jelly, candy, soup, and sandwich to list a few.

Medicinally the dandelion has served as a veritable drugstore. It has been used alone, or in combination with other herbs, to treat many ailments. Among them are diseases of the bladder, spleen, kidney, liver, pancreas, skin, heart, lungs, and stomach.

And there are, of course, the games and toys of adults and children reflected in names like "wishes" and "blowball." Whether it is to test a lover's fidelity, send a message to someone, or ask "does mother want me," blowball holds an answer, while its stems make curls for little girls and wonderfully squeaky tooters for little boys.

MULLEIN
Verbascum thapsus L.

Knowing that boys once considered mullein an acceptable behind-the-barn smoke, it is tempting to imagine that some parents were willing to overlook occasional infractions of "no-smoking" rules in hopes that there was some truth to an old Navajo belief that smoking mullein would do away with any tendencies to use bad language or to think bad thoughts.

Though their youngsters sometimes smoked mullein during covert sorties into the apparent pleasures of adulthood, the elders smoked it openly, in pipes or rolled into cigarettes, to relieve irritated mucous membranes, asthma, and spasmodic coughing. And today some claim a step in the direction of improved health by recommending a smoke made from mullein mixed with other favored herbs as a replacement for tobacco.

The plant was not reserved for smoking. In the Ozarks, for example, the leaves were soaked in hot vinegar and used as poultices to ease the pain of birdshot wounds and to make removal of the pellets easier and less painful. And it is said that in South Carolina farmers placed great quantities of the dried plant in barns to keep mice away from grain stored there.

If the fact that mullein is a plant with hair of its own is taken as a sign that it will be helpful in the care of human hair, it is no surprise to learn that a tea of mullein flowers was once used as a rinse in the belief that it would keep blonde hair golden. For the old folks the plant was burned and the ashes made into a soap which was supposed to return gray hair to its original color.

The hair of the plant was used as more than a sign. It was patiently scraped from the leaves and made into wicks for lamps and candles before cotton was introduced. Hummingbirds are said to take the fine velvet of mullein as a lining for their tiny nests.

PURSLANE
Portulaca oleracea L.

It may have been known as "the blessed vegetable" in Medieval times, but in more recent times purslane has acquired a reputation as "that cussed weed."

President Grant, during a visit to Charles Dudley Warner's vegetable garden, is supposed to have said that a necessity of civilization was to get rid of rats and pusley. Warner couldn't have agreed more, since he considered the plant a strangler of strawberries and possessed of a moral perversity which made it grow more the more it was interfered with by his efforts to root it out.

Though Warner may have broken his back trying to keep purslane from strangling his strawberries, others let it grow freely and even cultivated it. Joseph Cocannouer, in *Weeds: Guardians of the Soil*, described how one farmer decided to let the pusley grow in his cornfield because he believed the weed's roots opened up the soil and helped the corn to grow. And there are those who have regularly harvested purslane and used it as a vegetable, as a pickle, or in soups and salads.

Walter Beebe Wilder's grandfather let purslane grow until its stems made a half-acre look as if it were covered with a red haze. After that he saw that it appeared on the family dinner table so often that everyone became nauseated at the sight of it. Thoreau was more conservative. From his cornfield he gathered, boiled and salted just enough of the plant to provide him with several satisfactory dinners.

For all the sleepless nights its presence may have caused some gardeners, purslane has been included in lists of herbal medicines as a cure for sleeplessness and, as if to insure an even sounder sleep, the plant was often scattered around beds to protect superstitious sleepers from evil spirits.

WOOD SORREL
Oxalis stricta L.

Because wood sorrel was looked upon as a charm against snakes and other poison-dealers, it has been said that soldiers used to tie sprigs of the plant to their sword arms before going into battle and, having done so, felt themselves protected against enemies who had dark and secret ways of killing.

At the same time their ladies might have been using wood sorrel to spruce-up some of their best linens. Oxalic acid, which gives the juice of sorrel a sour taste and helps account for the name "sour grass," has long been used as a stain remover. The plant may have been called "ladies' sorrel" because it was used by women in this way, but the word "lady," uncapitalized as part of a plant name, is more often used to describe a plant with delicate (ladylike) features.

"Pickle grass" is another name which can be attributed to the sourness and the fact that the small seedpods are sometimes called pickles suggests food uses for the plant.

There is at least one other species of *Oxalis* on the islands *(Oxalis europaea)* and both are edible, though poisonous properties of the sour acid make it unwise to eat large quantities of either. Wood sorrel has been used in soups, salads, beverages, desserts, and as a thirst-quencher for hikers.

As a cloverlike plant with leaflets in groups of three, wood sorrel belongs with clover and medick, each of which is sometimes called the true Shamrock of St. Patrick. Certain as advocates of each may be that theirs is the one-and-only, the identity of the patron saint's plant remains a mystery. In 1892 and 1893, for example, a survey was conducted in Ireland of persons who were certain they knew what the "true Shamrock" was. White clover was nominated by 19 people, lesser trefoil by 12, purple clover by 2, and spotted medick by 2. No mention at all was made of wood sorrel.

CHICKWEED
Stellaria media Cyrill

Chickweed is a plant which makes a display of its sensitivity to darkness and bad weather. At night the tender buds of new shoots are protected by upper surfaces of leaves which fold over them with the coming of darkness.

On rainy days chickweed will not open its blossoms and, after particularly heavy rains, seems too weak even to raise its head, so the blossoms face down and it may be several days before they turn toward the sun once more.

The eyes of countrymen have not been blind to these things and common chickweed has found a place in folklore.

If chickweed's leaves are fully expanded,
fair weather is sure to follow.

When chickweed closes its blossoms,
the traveler should put on his raingear.

The rain will not last long if chickweed
flowers remain half-open.

If chickweed flowers remain open all night,
the weather will be wet next day.

As· with the discovery of uses for other wild plants, that for chickweed is marked by little surprises. In a description of chickweed as a plant whose mineral-rich leaves and stems make a good tonic for general upsets and an ointment which is good for skin ailments, there is no surprise. The same will be found in many herbals. But it *is* a surprise when the author adds that the ointment is also good for fur ailments and we discover that the description we have been reading is one of herbal medicines for pet rats and mice.

Chickweed is used far less today than it was when bundles of the plant were hawked on city streets for use in salads or as a cooked vegetable or in teas and home-remedies, yet some of today's ambitious dealers in roots and herbs give it a market value of $7.00 per pound — retail.

DAISY
Chrysanthemum leucanthemum L.

No small quantity of daisy seed is said to have come to our shores during Revolutionary times when it was brought from Germany in fodder destined for the horses of General Burgoyne. Since the earliest days of our colonization it has arrived as stowaway by one means or another and has flourished to the delight of many and to the distress of as many more.

Though daisies are beautiful plants, they are not appreciated in farmers' fields where they have a tendency to "take-over," to decrease production and thereby lower the value of any crop in which they are allowed to grow unchecked. In spite of it, the daisy succeeded in becoming the state flower of North Carolina.

It is a plant which everyone soon learns to recognize and "she loves me, she loves me not" seems to accompany introduction to the flower almost automatically. Although its use as an instrument of prophecy is most familiarly known by those words, there have been times when someone, apparently trying to improve chances of a favorable outcome, has altered the words. One variation used by petal-plucking seekers of information is "this year, next year, sometime, never." Whatever the final petal says is what the future holds, be it love, fame, or fortune one wishes to divine.

Daisies are also taken as symbols of innocence or fidelity and behind each symbol are stories. It has been said, for example, that every child who dies unborn or aborning returns to earth as a new flower. One mother, mourning a stillborn child, was told by the king's ladies to mourn no more, for the child had become a beautiful flower with silver petals surrounding a golden center. The flower, of course, was a daisy. From such fabled origins symbols of innocence and others have been derived.

JIMSONWEED
Datura stramonium L.

On walking the Boston Harbor Islands, it might easily be decided that one has stumbled upon a haven for witches if Jimsonweed is used as a clue.

In earlier times, when witchery was an everyday sort of thing, no self-respecting witch would have been without the plant. Among other things, it was one source of "flight-power," a ticket to what might be called a "trip" today. Properly understood, it could be used for high flights or low, fast flights or slow. Such flights have been described as joyous by some who have experimented with the broomstick weed. At the same time, they have been described as being accompanied by feelings that the body was falling apart and that death was just a hair's-breadth away, as indeed it was.

At least one author has surmised that grounded witches, with time on their hands and a need for some quick cash, might have exercised entrepreneurial talents by taking advantage of the plant's reported aphrodisiac properties to prepare little love potions for sale on the side.

Jimsonweed's association with witches may have been the best weed repellent around during the days when it was open season on women of such wickedness. All were sure to keep a close eye on the lawn to see that it remained clear of any sign of the plant. After all, what young lady in her right mind wanted to risk burning as a witch simply because some weed considered her yard a nice place to take root?

Jimsonweed is a beautiful plant whose foul-smelling leaves have proved no deterrent to children with the dangerous habit of sucking pretty blossoms or sampling sweet-tasting seeds. For all of its high-flying potential and fascinating history, it is a dangerous and powerfully narcotic weed which any wise island visitor will avoid as he would the fabled hypnotic eye of a deadly serpent.

PLANTAIN
Plantago major L.

Farmers once called plantain "fireweed" and used it to help decide when to put hay into the barn. Any moisture produced from a violently twisted plantain leaf was interpreted as meaning that the hay was still too green and should be allowed to dry longer to reduce chances of spontaneous combustion in the loft.

As a cow has been said to act as its own physician by eating pokeweed, so has a frog been said to find a plantain leaf to chew on immediately after being bitten by a spider and, by so doing, to have saved itself from any painful and poisonous consequences.

Superstitious people used to protect themselves from being bitten by snakes and other poisonous creatures by carrying pieces of plantain root around with them. Should they be bitten anyway, there was some comfort in the idea that a poultice of plantain leaves was a sure-fire remedy and the name "snakeweed" comes from that belief.

The astrologically minded used plantain, as an herb of Venus, to probe the future of a love match. To set the process of divination in motion a flowering stalk of plantain was picked for each member of a pair of lovers, all of the opened blossoms were removed, and the stalks were wrapped in a dock leaf and placed under a rock. When the sun next rose the packet was retrieved, opened, and the state of the stalks was said to foretell the future for the match. If both stalks had newly opened blossoms the future was believed to hold a mutual exchange of love. If only one, or neither, of the stalks held new blossoms the match was supposed to be doomed, for love would be no more than one-sided if it existed at all.

Among its more familiar uses, plantain has provided seed to feed birds. Children have used its flower stalks as toys, the young leaves have been used as people-food, and different parts of the plant have been used to treat such things as ulcers, tumors, piles, fevers, and bites from mad dogs.

POKE
Phytolacca americana L.

Weeds have been accused of all sorts of terrible things like ruining lawns, sousing birds, and knocking animals galley-west. Sometimes there is a touch of truth in the accusations but in 1867, when a farmer writing from Fort Independence tried to blame the appearance of a particular illness in his cows on their having eaten some weed peculiar to Castle Island, the author of *Facts for Farmers* did not hesitate to reply that it was because the farmer's animals had *not* been eating a certain weed. He then proceeded to describe how, if the cows had been eating pokeweed, a common pastoral antidote and cure for an unhealthy condition of bovine udders known as "garget," they would probably never have become sick.

The plant's use in treating that condition is the source of "garget" as a common name. So popular was poke as a medicinal for assorted animal ills that farmers in Vermont were once willing to pay $2.00 per pound for the dried root while others, exercising the legendary Yankee thrift and ingenuity, made certain a patch of the weed was always growing in their barnyards so that the cattle could act as their own physicians.

Good as the root may have been for animal ills, poke has always been poisonous for human beings. The sprouts of early spring are well known for their edibility as greens but the mature plant, once it has started to develop its characteristic red coloring, is not safe to eat. And although the berries are said to have been used to make tarts and pies, any recipes for the same remain hidden and wise persons will not use the berries as food.

A cart-before-the-horse suggestion has it that poke got its name because the plant's leaves were worn as emblems by supporters of James K. Polk during the Presidential campaign of 1844. Aside from the fact that the spellings are not alike, "poke" was old long before "Polk" was ever born.

QUEEN ANNE'S LACE
Daucus carota L.

Where jimsonweed has been companion to witches in their shadowed coves, the wild carrot has more commonly been associated with noble things in the court of James I and Queen Anne of England. There the large leaves of wild carrot were worn as ornaments in the hair of ladies of the court, or in hats, or pinned to sleeves in place of feathers. So highly were the leaves valued for this purpose that the tops were cut away and carefully tended in saucers of water until the feathery foliage attained a desired size and fullness. To assure a constant supply, quantities of them were wrapped in damp moss and carefully stored away until needed. Some believe the name Queen Anne's lace comes from such uses.

Some people look to the delicate, flat-topped clusters of blossoms for an explanation of the name. Where the plants grow undisturbed, the flowers may blanket whole fields with a coverlet which seems more closely akin to the finest white lace of a queen than any leaf of green.

In its own way, the wild carrot may be as dangerous as the jimsonweed. Relatives which closely resemble the wild carrot have been mistaken for it with disastrous results. They include water hemlock *(Cicuta maculata)* and poison hemlock *(Conium maculatum)* which was used to execute the philosopher Socrates. It is one good example of a reason for the forager's rule which says "never put a plant in your mouth until you are certain what it is and that it is harmless." Permit no doubt. The wild carrot is good to eat, but its look-alikes may be deadly.

Queen Anne's lace is also a plant of fancy. In the center of many of its blossoms is a tiny floret, rose or deep purple in color, which is said, by some, to be the queen in the middle of her lace and, by others, to be a drop of blood which fell there when the queen pricked her finger.

SHEPHERD'S PURSE
Capsella bursa-pastoris (L.) Medic.

There are those who say the name pick-purse was given to this plant because it robbed the farmer of the goodness of his land. It is a hard explanation to understand from the small, easily controlled specimens usually found on the islands or almost anywhere else in the area. But it has been cited as a plant which harbors a fungus said to cause clubroot in cabbage, cauliflower, and radish and that might help explain the name from a farmer's point of view.

There is an English child's game — more like a trick — in which the plant and its seedpods are held out to be taken hold of by an unwary friend. When the plant is grasped, the pods break open, the seeds scatter, and the trickster shouts "you've broken your mother's heart." In Switzerland the unfortunate one is accused of stealing a purse of gold from his mother and father.

Shepherd's purse is a peppery salad plant and was once sold as a vegetable in the markets around Philadelphia. If the reports are accurate, specimens grown there must have made midgets of any we are apt to find. In 1821, for example, it was reported to the Horticultural Society of London that shepherd's purse from cultivated spots near Philadelphia grew to a size and succulence scarcely to be believed without seeing the plants.

The seeds were at one time collected by California Indians and ground to make a flour, but the seeds are better known as food for small wild and caged birds.

Shepherd's purse has not escaped the attention of herbal healers. It was once believed that jaundice could be relieved if shepherd's purse were just bound to the wrists or to the soles of the feet. Teas, poultices, and ointments made from shepherd's purse have been used to stop ringing in the ears and bleeding of noses. They were held in high regard for stopping hemorrhages of all kinds and during the First World War, when the plants usually used in making medicines for those purposes were not available from Germany, shepherd's purse was used as a substitute.

YARROW
Achillea millefolium L.

The common names for yarrow indicate that it has been used more as a medicine than for anything else. The more we read about it, though, the more uses we discover.

The coarse leaves, for example, have been used as playthings by children who, it is said, used to scrape them across their faces to cause a tingling sensation. Some believe the name Devil's nettle arose from this use while others say that the name, along with Devil's plaything, came from the plant's use as a fortune-teller.

It was once believed that the image of a future husband or wife could be called forth if one tied an ounce of yarrow inside a square of flannel and, after saying the proper words before going to bed, placed it under the pillow.

The leaves have been used in soups and salads in northern France and Germany and have served as tobacco and to make beer in Sweden.

Among the ways in which yarrow is said to have been used medicinally are two seemingly contradictory ones which gave it the name "nosebleed." The leaves, rolled up, thrust into the nose and twisted, were used to cause nosebleeds in the belief that migraine could be thus relieved. On the other hand, the leaves were also used to pack nasal passages in order to stop bleeding. Yarrow tea is supposed to be good for colds and to break a fever by increasing perspiration. The same tea was supposed to be a good cure for baldness if the head were washed with it. Yarrow has been used as a cure for rheumatism and it was once believed that chewing the fresh leaves would cure toothache.

And yarrow is an effective repeller of ants. Pick it at the right time, strew it where the unwanted ants congregate and the problem will be ended.

LADY'S THUMB
Polygonum persicaria L.

"Once upon a time" those who saw the spots on the leaves of this plant as red and heart-shaped took it as a sign that the plant was meant to be used in the treatment of heart problems and called it "heart's-ease." Those who saw redness, but only irregular spots where others saw the shape of a heart, said the plant must have been growing at the foot of Christ's cross and the red spots could be nothing less than dried drops of blood.

For others the spots were leaden, shapeless blotches of gray, like little fingerprint bruises. It was as if the Virgin Mary had pinched the leaves and it was taken as a sign that the plant was to be used as a treatment for bruises. They called it Lady's thumb.

Some people with perhaps a more earthy character, looked closely at other parts of the plant and the way it grew. They noted its red and knobby joints and gave it names like "red-shanks" and "red-knees" and "knotweed," names which have come down to us in the Latin name *Polygonum*, meaning "many knees," and may explain why the plant was believed to be useful in the treatment of arthritis.

Lady's thumb has also been used as a gargle for sore mouths, to take away toothaches, and to keep flies away from sores on farm animals. Edwin Rollin Spencer suggested that farmers should welcome the weed and use it in another way. He believed that Lady's thumb, weedy relative of the soil-building buckwheat, should be encouraged because it would grow better on poor soil than its cultivated cousin and, as a result, would return more fertilizer to the land. And, though Lady's thumb is not usually thought of as a plant for flower gardens, the *Cyclopedia of American Horticulture* (1906 ed.) said that it was once marketed by seedsmen as a suitable background plant.

Seeds of Lady's thumb, not so peppery as those from some of its relatives, have been ground into flour or pressed into cakes for human consumption. They have also been collected as food for birds.

MILKWEED
Asclepias syriaca L.

Fibers from stalks of milkweed plants have been used by American Indians to make string and rope. In France and Russia a glossy white thread has been made from them, but those from the mature pods, the fibers which give us the name "silkweed," are too short to be used by themselves and have had to be mixed with wool, cotton, flax, and silk for spinning. Used alone, they are excellent stuffing for children's toys and beds. Pillows stuffed with fibers from the pods are soft and coolest of the cool for summer use. Paper, felt, a kind of muslin, plastic, drugs, oils, and insulating boards have all been made from milkweed.

Reference is often made to a Canadian practice of making sugar from the milkweed flowers. Peter Kalm, sent by the Swedish government to report on the natural resources of North America in 1748, described the process as one of boiling down the dew-covered flowers, but those who have tried it report little success.

The white sap has been successfully converted into a chewing gum. Children in the midwest used to break the midribs of the large leaves, allow the oozing juice to harden for a few minutes and then collect and chew it. Indians of southern California did much the same thing, letting large quantities of the sap harden by the campfires overnight. A bitterness present when the gum was first chewed soon disappeared.

At one time the sap was also used to remove warts and moles. Various preparations of roots, juices, and seeds have been used in medicines believed helpful in treating asthma, dropsy, dysentery, epilepsy, lung and chest problems, enteritis, typhus, and nervousness. There was a time, before the "pill," when Indian women of Quebec used an infusion of the pounded roots to induce a temporary sterility.

SHEEP SORREL
Rumex acetosella L.

If you are attacked by a small, pugnacious, coppery-orange butterfly in your walks around the islands, look for the "little vinegar plant." Chances are you've been discovered by an American Copper, a common butterfly in this part of the country, whose larva, finding nothing more to its taste than *Rumex acetosella*, eventually became the butterfly with a temperament as acid as the plant which fed it. Were it good for nothing else, the "little vinegar plant" would still be valued as a primary source of nourishment for the pretty insect which does not hesitate to attack anything which moves within its range.

Hikers, too, favor the leaves of the acid-flavored plant as thirst-quenchers. Also known as sheep sorrel, the plant is recommended as one for soups and salads, as one whose chopped leaves provide a pleasant tartness when added to cottage cheese or sprinkled onto an omelet, and as a seasoning for fish, rice, and potatoes. Sheep sorrel has even been used in jams, jellies, and pies.

Superstitious folks in New Brunswick, Canada, once believed that eating the plant would give them head lice, but the only real risks seem to be two which rarely produce any damaging results. Handling the leaves has produced mild skin irritation in persons who are especially sensitive, and eating too much of the plant may result in poisoning by the oxalic acid which it contains (see *Oxalis*).

Peter Kalm wrote about another use for sheep sorrel. He explained how a material to be dyed could be given a durable black color by boiling it with leaves of sorrel, drying it and then reboiling it with logwood and copperas.

BURDOCK
Arctium minus Bernh.

When it comes to seed production, burdock makes a piker of amaranth. A single burdock plant may produce as many as 400,000 seeds and distribute them widely by attaching to every passer-by, be it man or animal, those pesky little burs so familiar to wanderers through autumn fields. Fortunately, all of those seeds don't live to produce new plants. For years, though, enough of them have regularly survived so that mankind, true to his nature, has allowed curiosity free-rein to experiment and develop all sorts of uses for the plant.

As an example of a toy-plant, burdock is used by children, even today, to make baskets, chains, tiny houses, little people, birds, and animals. Its bristly burs serve as safe substitutes for darts when thrown against a bullseye drawn on a piece of felt. And mischievous boys seem always to have courted the wrath of mothers by tossing a bur or two into the hair of a nearby friend. Masks to cover the faces of actors in ancient Greece were once made from the large, heart-shaped, leaves of burdock and from the practice comes the name *personata*, a Latin word meaning "masked" or "clad in a mask."

Where a proper use of yarrow was supposed to make it possible to create the vision of a future spouse, burdock burs once provided means whereby young ladies might check on a lover's fidelity. By picking a bur while thinking about the lover in question and then having a friend throw the bur against her skirt, a young woman could rest assured of the lover's fidelity if the bur stuck. Failure to stick was interpreted as a sign that the lover was untrue.

The roots of burdock boiled with fat meat and eaten were said to be aphrodisiac by some and, by others, to produce just the opposite effect.

As a medicinal plant the list of uses for burdock is long and varied. It includes curing of toothaches, treatment of sties and snakebites, coughs, asthma, assorted lung and chest problems, gout, rheumatism, stomachache, bruises, swellings, burns, and skin diseases.

CHICORY
Cichorium intybus L.

Adulteration of food is nothing new in this country. Before the Civil War coffee was being adulterated with roasted and ground things like peas, sweet potatoes, corn, and cotton seed. During the Civil War, when good coffee was too expensive for most pocketbooks, chicory was used as an adulterant superior to others and grocers proposed that its use kept even the most expensive coffee within the reach of almost everyone. Not only was it possible to reduce the price of the costly product by adulterating it with chicory, but the chicory itself was promoted as improving the final brew by deepening its color and enriching its flavor.

By the time the war ended, though, chicory had become associated with deprivation and hardship and was, for many, a thing to be accepted only in the greatest of emergencies. Nevertheless, there were others who had come to appreciate chicory in their coffee so much that 7,000,000 pounds a year were imported during one period and, just before World War I, 2,250,000 pounds of European-grown root were being shipped into the country. Where those who did not care for chicory in their coffee said it was poor-folks' stuff, those who savored it said that the American-grown root was not good enough and went on using imported roots while efforts to grow, process, and market chicory at home were not as successful as hoped.

In true weed fashion, though, chicory refused to be denied. It has continued to multiply with little, if any, help until it can be found growing wild in a broad band across the middle of the country from the East Coast to the West Coast.

Were it only able to sit across the table from some of those who look down their noses at it, chicory might just improve its own image, for it is one of those plants whose seeds, dropped secretly into food, are rumored to have the power of generating love.

COMMON MALLOW
Malva neglecta Wallr.

Because it is low-growing and not a very conspicuous plant, the common mallow is easily overlooked. This could well account for the specific name *neglecta*, which is Latin for "disregarded" or "neglected." Compared to the many uses to which some of the other island plants have been put, this one might certainly be considered neglected, but mallow's inconspicuous character has not kept it from the sharp eyes of curious children. Their use of its seed capsules as play-food, and a resemblance to tiny wheels of cheese, have given the plant the name of "doll-cheeses."

We can only speculate that some young woman or man, long-suffering from an open collar, a floppy cuff, or the gaping front of blouse or shirt, looked with fond rememberings of buttoned-up days upon the form and size of the fruit before christening mallow the "shirt-button plant" in noble effort to impress a negligent helpmeet.

Gathered when the plant is young and tender, mallow makes a good potherb and was once cultivated for that purpose by the Egyptians. The fruits have been used as hikers' nibbles, pickled in brine or vinegar, and added to soup and salad to provide snap. The dried leaves make a good tea and are reported to have been sold commercially as such in the midwest.

As the name "mallow" suggests, the plant is member of a family which includes the marshmallow. The family, which also includes the hollyhock, rose of Sharon, and cotton, is one with valued medicinal properties. A poultice of the steeped fresh leaves of common mallow is said to be helpful in relieving the pain and swelling of bee stings as well as that of some other skin irritations.

PART II
FIELD GUIDE

IN THE FIELD

The twenty-five plants with which the book is concerned form a good core around which to plan a plant-hunting trip to the islands. Some of the plants are common enough to be almost certainly found, and so guarantee a degree of success. Discovery of others is less certain and elements of suspense and challenge are thus provided for. Since it cannot be guaranteed that all of the plants will be found on any one island, there is a built-in opportunity, or excuse, to visit several of the islands.

The guide is designed to help you locate and identify the plants in the field. It begins with a table indicating islands from which each of the twenty-five plants has been reported. This is followed by drawings and descriptions of the plants and accompanied by additional notes and suggestions about where you might look for them on Gallops, Lovells, Georges, and Thompson's, four of the most readily accessible islands. Places to look, as pinpointed on maps of the four islands, are meant to be taken only as suggestions and real-life wanderings will probably cross and recross anything drawn on the maps. Also, a glossary is included to help with unfamiliar words.

Time and place to begin to know the island plants are spring, summer, and fall out-of-doors. It is then and there that the plants can be found in quantity and seen in their most recognizable forms. The most valuable piece of equipment for your plant hunting trip will probably be a small backpack, like those seen around campuses when schools are in session. With it you will be able to carry things like a field guide, hand lens (magnifying glass), notebook, pencils, knife, insect repellent, sun-tan lotion, band-aids, sweater, rain gear, lunch, and water. The pack will be small enough to make you think twice about whatever else you may want to put into it, but large enough to insure that you will be able to take everything you will really need. In addition to what goes into your pack and onto your back, you will probably be glad to have a cap with visor, sunglasses, and waterproof shoes comfortable for walking and climbing.

At the very least, in making your plans, give careful consideration to the items mentioned. Sun can be glaring on sand and open water. It beats down mercilessly on exposed places. Island weather is fickle and warm may become cold, sunny may become rainy quickly and unexpectedly. Trudging along beaches, over hills, across fields, through thickets and into marshes is guaranteed to tire feet and whet appetites.

Be sure to take a notebook and make notes, lots of them, and perhaps even some sketches. Don't be tricked by excitement and novelty into believing that you will not forget anything about the plant-hunting experience or any of the people you may meet as you tour the islands. There is every chance that by the time Christmas arrives you won't be able to recall some of the best moments without help from a few memory-joggers.

Although there is no substitute for conscientious planning, it is reassuring to know that the four islands specified, as well as some of the others, are occupied by one or more persons who are invariably friendly and always available as first or last resort when help and information are needed.

If this sounds like preparation for something like an African safari, there is good reason. Being well prepared is the best way to be sure that you will enjoy an island trip and that the memories collected will be the sort you will entertain with pleasure during winter days when island adventures are little more than dream-stuff.

For up-to-date information about the islands and how to get there, call the Metropolitan District Commission's Recreation Department at (617) 727-5250. An assortment of helpful information will be found in *All About the Boston Harbor Islands*, by Emily and David Kales. The *Boston Harbor Islands Comprehensive Plan*, published in 1972 by the Massachusetts Department of Natural Resources, is a goldmine of ideas about the future of the islands and is liberally sprinkled with past history, natural history, maps, and pictures of each island.

SELECTED PLANTS AND THE ISLANDS FROM WHICH THEY HAVE BEEN REPORTED

	GALLOPS	GEORGES	LOVELLS	THOMPSON'S	BUMPKIN	CALF	GRAPE	GREAT BREWSTER	GREEN	LANGLEY	LITTLE BREWSTER	MIDDLE BREWSTER	OUTER BREWSTER	PEDDOCKS	RACCOON	RAGGED	RAINSFORD	SARAH	SHEEP	SLATE	SPECTACLE
GREEN, YELLOW-GREEN																					
Amaranth	●																●				
Cattail			●	●				●				●									
Curly dock	●	●	●	●	●		●	●	●	●	●	●		●	●		●		●	●	●
Lambsquarters	●	●	●				●	●						●		●					
Mugwort	●	●	●	●			●	●	●								●		●		
Poison ivy	●		●	●	●		●		●	●	●			●	●	●	●	●			
YELLOW																					
Butter and eggs		●	●	●	●			●			●	●	●	●		●	●	●	●	●	
Dandelion	●	●	●	●	●	●	●	●		●	●	●		●			●		●		●
Mullein	●	●	●	●	●		●	●			●		●	●	●		●		●		●
Purslane	●							●	●	●		●							●		
Wood sorrel	●	●		●	●																
WHITE																					
Chickweed	●	●	●		●									●			●				
Daisy	●	●	●	●	●		●							●			●				
Jimsonweed	●	●	●	●			●	●	●												
Plantain	●	●	●	●				●	●		●			●							
Poke		●		●	●		●									●					
Queen Anne's lace	●	●	●	●	●		●	●						●					●		
Shepherd's purse		●	●											●							
Yarrow	●	●	●	●	●	●	●	●			●	●	●	●	●		●	●	●	●	●
PINK, RED-ORANGE																					
Lady's thumb	●		●	●				●													
Milkweed	●	●	●	●	●		●	●							●	●	●		●	●	
Sheep sorrel	●	●	●	●	●		●	●			●	●			●	●	●	●	●	●	●
PURPLE, BLUE, LILAC																					
Burdock		●	●	●	●			●	●		●			●			●				
Chicory	●	●	●	●	●		●	●				●		●			●				
Common mallow		●		●					●		●	●									

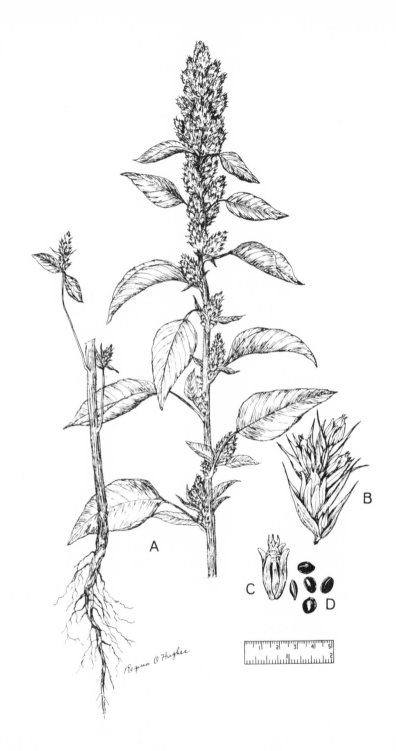

Amaranthus retroflexus L.   Redroot pigweed.   *A*, Habit— × 0.5;   *B*, pistillate
spikelet— × 5;   *C*, utricle— × 5;   *D*, seeds— × 3.

AMARANTH

Amaranthus retroflexus L.

Common names: pigweed, flower-of-love, careless weed, tumbleweed, wild-beet

Description: Family: AMARANTHACEAE (Amaranth Family).

Source: Naturalized from tropical America.

Duration: Annual.

Habitat: Disturbed areas, cultivated fields, vegetable gardens.

Habit: Stems erect; branched in the upper portions; rough; somewhat hairy; up to 6-feet tall.

Leaves: Alternate; simple; long-petioled; gray-green; wavy; ovate toward the base, 3–6 inches long; more lanceolate toward top of plant.

Flowers: Green; small; crowded into spikes in leaf axils and in dense panicles at ends of branches. Blossoms August to October.

Reproduces: By seeds.

Amaranth is sometimes called pigweed because pigs find it so much to their taste that they will eat it at every opportunity and never seem to get enough. Cows, on the other hand, have been known to be poisoned by it because the plant has a way of accumulating an excess of nitrates under some conditions and cattle which eat it may become bloated. As a result, amaranth is sometimes listed as a poisonous plant.

As an annual weed of cultivated places, and one which germinates easily and grows rapidly with just a little bit of encouragement, amaranth has provided anyone who hates the plant with a fairly easy means to destroy it. Those who know say that it is only necessary to disturb the soil, wait for the amaranth seeds to germinate, and then hand-weed or hoe the plants under before they can go to seed. The exercise will quicken the heart of any weed-hater with the realization that the destruction of each seedling may save his garden from nearly 200,000 seeds which would have been freely scattered had the plant been allowed to mature.

It would not be surprising to find specimens growing almost anywhere on the islands that the land had been recently disturbed and left to develop untended.

Amaranth has been seen . . .
. . . growing in the area of the picnic tables near the wharf on Gallops Island.

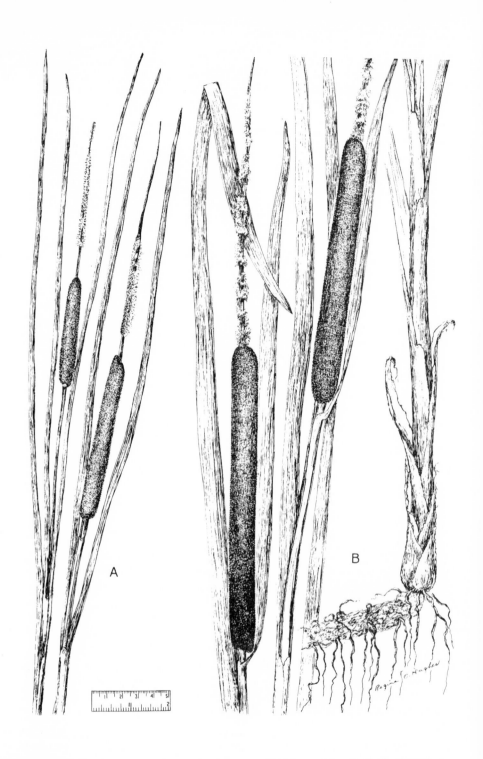

Typha angustifolia L.   Narrowleaf cattail.   *A*, Habit— × 0.5;   *B, Typha latifolia* L.
Common cattail.   Habit— × 0.5.

CATTAIL

Typha latifolia L.

Common names: cat-o-nine-tails, chimney sweeps, reed-mace, water torch, mat-rush

Description:

Family:	TYPHACEAE (Cattail Family).
Source:	Native to the United States.
Duration:	Perennial.
Habitat:	Fresh-water marshes, shallow water and wet waste places.
Habit:	Stems erect; stout; 3–8 feet tall.
Leaves:	Flat; ¼–1 inch broad; pale to grayish-green; sheathe stem; may grow taller than stem.
Flowers:	In two-part spike at end of stem; top part male (staminate) yellow-green, 3–5 inches long; bottom part female (pistillate) green becoming dark brown, 1–8 inches long, ½–1½ inches thick; the two parts usually touch one another. Blossoms May to July.
Reproduces:	From creeping rhizomes and airborne seeds.

Those great migrating insect travelers, the monarch butterflies, flit through patches of island milkweed and lay their eggs. The larvae feed on these plants and their beautiful green, gold-studded chrysalides will sometimes be found hanging from the undersides of the leaves.

Black-eyed susans may harbor insects, including "loopers" in twig-like poses, and daisy stems may be measured bit-by-bit by the geometrid inch-worms. The wooly-bear caterpillar whose coat is said to foretell harsh or mild winters, relishes plantain leaves while the "gold-bug," an insect which can change its colors, is common on the bindweed, and dozens of bees and butterflies visit the yarrow.

Stories of insects associated with island plants can be as fascinating as those of the plants themselves. Viceroy mimics the monarch and so is said to be protected from attacks by birds. The width of a wooly-bear's black band is a weather indicator for country folk. One of the caterpillar's common names is "hedgehog" and comes from the way it curls up and lies motionless when disturbed. The slang phrase "to caterpillar," meaning "to yield to the unavoidable without complaint," is also said to have come from the wooly-bear's behavior.

Cattails, too, can serve as reminders that insects use plants as much as people do. The leaves sometimes swarm with aphids, are punctured by snout beetles, or mined and webbed by an assortment of caterpillars. At least three different types of caterpillars are known to live in long water-filled borrows deep within the stems.

Cattails have been seen . . .

. . . at the center of Thompson's Island around the old skating pond.

. . . at the west end of Peddocks Island.

Rumex crispus L.   Curly dock.   *A,* Habit—×0.5;   *B,* Fruit, *a,* surrounded by persistent calyx, *b,* showing 3 valves— × 3.5;   *C,* achene— × 5.

CURLY DOCK

Rumex crispus L.

Common names: coffee weed, pike plant, yellow dock, sour dock, bitter dock

Description:

Family:	POLYGONACEAE (Buckwheat Family).
Source:	Naturalized from Eurasia.
Duration:	Perennial.
Habitat:	Old fields and roadsides.
Habit:	Stems erect; single or in groups; smooth; branched above; up to 3-feet tall.
Leaves:	Rosette first year; alternate; simple; curly and wavy margins; lanceolate; 6–12 inches long; papery sheath surrounds stem at base of petiole.
Flowers:	Green becoming brown at maturity; tiny; long slender pedicels; in dense whorled clusters of ascending racemes at ends of branches. Blossoms June to September.
Reproduces:	By seeds.

Because a rusty raggedness makes it a stand-out in early fall and winter, curly dock is often quick to attract attention when showier plants have gone by. But arrangers of flowers begin the search early for useful plants and the growing season is still young when the curly dock first attracts their attention.

By June the collectors have begun to gather and dry the plant to preserve its greenness. As the year moves into summer and on to fall, they continue watching and picking and drying for color through what is called a touch-of-rose, then rust, then a light reddish-brown, and finally a deep seal-brown.

Flower arrangers see a use for curly dock's tall, coarse, and tattered figure in grand informal structures. But the plant can be taken apart, the arrangers say, and used less dramatically. It is then we discover that words like "warm" and "subtle" and "delicate" are not strangers to descriptions of curly dock. They are not words usually associated with such plants, but who is to say what others will see . . . even in a common weed.

Curly dock . . .

. . . is often one of the first plants an observant eye will notice in the field just beyond the pergola on Gallops Island.

. . . grows in the gun emplacements on Lovells Island.

. . . has been seen in the field south of the wharf on Georges Island.

. . . has been found in the vicinity of the wharf on Thompson's Island.

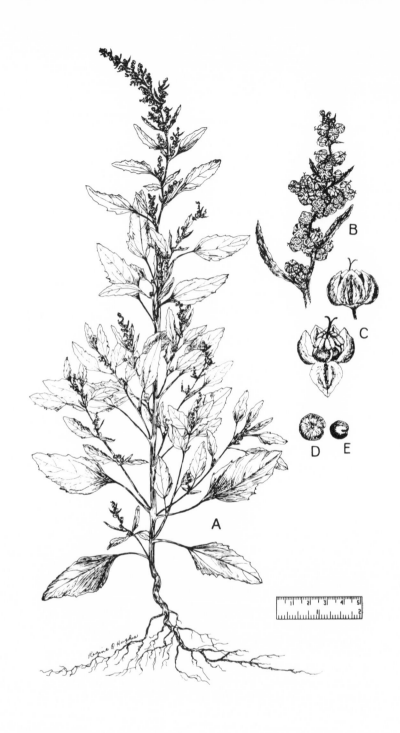

Chenopodium album L.   Common lambsquarters.   *A,* Habit, small plant;   *B,* floral spike— × 2.5;   *C,* flowers— × 7.5;   *D,* utricle— × 4;   *E,* seed— × 4.

LAMBSQUARTERS

Chenopodium album L.

Common names: goosefoot, wild spinach, frost blite, pigweed, wormseed

Description: Family: CHENOPODIACEAE (Goosefoot Family).

Source: Naturalized from Europe.

Duration: Annual.

Habitat: Gardens and waste ground.

Habit: Stems erect; branching above; smooth; 4–inches to 6–feet tall; occasionally streaked red.

Leaves: Alternate; simple; varying from broadly toothed, diamond-shaped (goosefoot), and petioled low down on the stem, to long, narrow, and sometimes sessile at the top; undersides frosty-green and mealy.

Flowers: Greenish; tiny; sessile; in dense, mealy spikes in leaf axils at top of plant. Blossoms June to October.

Reproduces: By seeds.

Years ago lambsquarters was much more popular as a food plant than it is today. One of its common names, "meld," is a good example how indications of past popularity and commonness are sometimes found in surprising forms. The present name of the English town of Melbourn, for example, was derived from its 10th-century name "Meldeburna," which meant "the stream where meld grows."

Lambsquarters is easily confused with either of two close relatives which are also found on the islands. One of them, *Atriplex patula* L., sometimes called seaside lambsquarters but more commonly known as orach, will be found along the beaches and on the salt marshes. It is a weaker plant than *Chenopodium album*, and more likely to sprawl than to grow upright. Orach's leaves are hastate (arrow-head in shape), while those of lambsquarters are not. The other cousin is *Chenopodium rubrum* L., coast blite. This plant has not the mealiness on the underside of its leaves, and grows on the salt marshes and in moist salty soils elsewhere.

Lambsquarters is a plant of gardens, cultivated fields, and dry wasteplaces. It has been seen . . .

  . . . along the slate-chip pathways of Gallops Island where the plant is small and obviously not its best self. Healthier plants will be found off to the side along the edges of the pathways.

  . . . in the field at the south end of Georges Island and along the stony pathways.

  . . . in the field east of the gym on Thompson's Island.

Artemisia vulgaris L.   Mugwort.   *A,* Habit— × 0.5;   *B,* enlarged leaves— × 1;
C, panicle— × 3;   *D,* flower head— × 4;   *E,* flowers— × 7.5;   *F,* achenes— × 5.

MUGWORT
Artemisia vulgaris L.

Common names: felon herb, wormwood, sailor's tobacco, grey-toad, St. John's plant.

Description:

Family:	COMPOSITAE (Composite Family).
Source:	Naturalized from Europe.
Duration:	Perennial.
Habitat:	Open sunny fields and in rubble-strewn lots.
Habit:	Stems erect; angular; branching; sometimes reddish; 4–6 feet tall.
Leaves:	Alternate; simple; pinnate; deeply lobed; 1–4½ inches long, 1¼–2¾ inches wide; smooth and dark green above; silvery below; lower leaves petioled; upper leaves sessile; strong chrysanthemum odor when crushed.
Flowers:	Gray-green; small; in spike-like clusters in leaf axils and at tops of stems. Blossoms July to September.
Reproduces:	By seeds and short rootstocks.

Mugwort is sometimes mistaken for common ragweed, especially early in the season when the plants are small. But the silvery undersides of mugwort's leaves and their chrysanthemum-like odor when crushed, quickly give away its identity.

It is also said that mugwort can be mistaken for mugwort, a confusing proposition which is sometimes supported by involved explanations to the effect that one variety stays in its place in the garden while the other rambles and eventually gets out of hand and abuses its welcome there.

Be that as it may, the one we are concerned with here is certainly unruly and unloved by those who favor well-controlled gardens . . . which is one way of calling a weed a weed. But in its place, this plant is not one without virtue. There are those who look with favor upon the way mugwort has of spreading its rootstocks and sending up new shoots until the unsightly litter of rubble-strewn city lots is beautifully covered with tall green screens which flash silver in summer breezes.

Mugwort has been seen . . .
  . . . on the slope near the pergola on Gallops Island and in the large clearing atop the island.
  . . . in the field at the south end of Georges Island.
  . . . in the gun emplacements on Lovells Island.
  . . . at the edge of the beach by the wharf on Thompson's Island.

Rhus radicans L.   Poison ivy.   *A*, Habit— × 0.5;   *B*, flower panicle— × 0.5;
C, flowers— × 4;   *D*, drupe— × 2.5;   *E*, stones— × 2.5;   *F*, aerial roots— × 2.5.

POISON IVY

Rhus radicans L.

Common names: three-leaved ivy, poison oak, mercury, markweed, cow-itch

Description:

Family:	ANACARDIACEAE (Cashew Family).
Source:	Native to the United States.
Duration:	Perennial.
Habitat:	Thickets, open woods, pastures.
Habit:	Stems woody; erect; shrubby or vine-like, climbing by means of aerial rootlets.
Leaves:	Alternate; compound with three large shiny or dull leaflets each 2–4 inches long; entire, toothed, or somewhat lobed; smooth or somewhat hairy.
Flowers:	Yellow-green; 5 petals; small; in open panicles up to four inches long from leaf axils. Blossoms May to July.
Fruit:	Hard gray drupes slightly less than ¼ inch in diameter.
Reproduces:	By seeds and creeping rootstocks.
Other:	All parts poisonous to touch.

Probably no plant is more generally recognized as harmful than poison ivy. Its victims have been said to far outnumber those of all other poisonous plants combined. It was not until 1895 that a true explanation of what caused the poisonous effects was offered by Dr. Franz Pfaff of Harvard. Before Dr. Pfaff's explanation, people believed the poisoning was caused by a volatile acid, mysterious exhalations from the plant, and even bacteria. It proved to be a slightly volatile oil, however.

All parts of the plant are poisonous to the touch of susceptible persons . . . stems, bark, leaves, flowers, fruits, roots . . . and may produce severe inflamation and blisters. As mentioned elsewhere, even smoke from fires in which poison ivy is being burned can cause some bad cases of dermatitis. "Leaflets three, let it be," is good advice to heed.

Poison ivy isn't an especially hard plant to find on the islands once one learns to recognize it, but it often seems to attract attention only when one is standing right in the middle of a flourishing growth of it. Slate Island is said to be particularly rich in the plant. Fortunately, poison ivy doesn't run rampant over most of the islands.

It can be seen . . .

. . . surrounding the haze of asparagus fronds at the base of the north bluff on Gallops Island.

. . . at the base of the "highlands," in the low wet thickets where woods yield to tall grasses that fringe the old tidal zone leading to Battery Tirrell on Lovells Island.

Linaria vulgaris Mill.   Yellow toadflax.   *A*, Habit— × 0.5;   *B*, flowers— × 0.75;
C, capsules— × 1.5;   *D*, seeds— × 5.

BUTTER AND EGGS
Linaria vulgaris Mill.

Common names: toadflax, snapdragon, flaxweed, gallwort, brideweed

Description: Family: SCROPHULARIACEAE (Figwort Family).

              Source: Naturalized from Europe.

              Duration: Perennial.

              Habitat: Old fields and disturbed areas.

              Habit: Stems erect; slender; smooth; not much branched; 1–3 feet tall.

              Leaves: Alternate; simple; entire; sessile; ½–1½ inches long; very narrow; blue-green.

              Flowers: Yellow and orange; snapdragon shape; appear in dense racemes at top of plants. Blossoms June to October.

              Reproduces: By seeds and creeping rootstocks.

When they are present, the blossoms of butter and eggs make it a hard plant to miss. The flowers resemble small yellow mouths with orange palates. The upper and lower lips can be separated and each blossom can be peeked into as if one were examining a toad's throat. The blossoms will snap shut when released, if they have been handled carefully. The name "rabbits," another for this plant, apparently came from the practice of children who took the blossoms between thumb and forefinger, looked at it, squeezed it gently, and were made to think of a bunny's snout or mouth by what they saw. The tension of this floral "jaw" is just enough to make it a bee's flower. Most other insects are too weak or lightweight to open the blossoms and get at the nectar.

Mention of teas made from wild plants often brings to mind visions of irate colonials and the alternatives they chose for their teas as part of the protest against the king's exorbitant tax. Rarely does mention of wild teas cause one to think of sick chickens, yet it was to revive spirits of ailing fowls that farmwives once laced henyard drinking water with an infusion made from leaves of toadflax.

Sometimes mistaken for a wild form of the domestic snapdragon, butter and eggs has been taken up and planted in home flower gardens to the later regret of the gardener, for the roots soon creep beyond any allotted space and must be dug out lest they take over the whole garden. Because butter and eggs reproduces by creeping roots, it often appears in patches along roadsides and fields.

Butter and eggs has been seen . . .

. . . along the edges of trails and in dry open fields where competition from taller and coarser plants is not too great.

. . . on many of the islands.

. . . in the fields at the northeast end of Thompson's Island and along the Southwest Trail near the root cellars.

Taraxacum officinale Weber.   Dandelion.   *A*, Habit— × 0.5;   *B*, flower— × 3;
C, achenes— × 7.5;   *D*, achenes with pappus— × 1.

DANDELION

Taraxacum officinale Weber

Common names: blowball, schoolboy clock, pissenlit, wishes, swine snout

Description:	Family:	COMPOSITAE (Composite Family).
	Source:	Naturalized from Europe.
	Duration:	Perennial.
	Habitat:	Found in sunny fields nearly everywhere.
	Habit:	Rosette of leaves with several long, hollow, smooth scapes.
	Leaves:	Basal; entire to toothed and lobed; 2–16 inches long; often with short soft hairs.
	Flowers:	Yellow; 1¼–2 inches broad at end of scape sometimes 24 inches long; solitary heads. Blossoms March to September (occasionally during the winter).
	Reproduces:	By seeds and new shoots from roots.
	Other:	Milky sap.

Though weeds harass men, as exemplified in part by chickweed, true and noble weeds do not stop there. They also war with one another. It is a quiet war and it goes on among island weeds as well as among weeds elsewhere. Dodder *(Cuscuta gronovii* Willd.*),* for example, has no chlorophyl to help in the manufacture of its own sugar and so uses sets of small suckers to parasitize plants around which it twines. The buttercups secrete poisonous substances into the soil from their roots which act as depressants on plants which grow near them. Canada fleabane *(Erigeron canadensis* L.*)* carries the battle right to its own family and seedlings are stunted by dead roots of older plants of the same species.

Having a great appetite for iron, nitrogen, calcium, copper, and other nutrients gives the dandelion a fair start toward starving its vegetable neighbors. And the plant uses the nourishment, in part, to develop and lay down a smothering array of leaves which keeps out both light and water to further hinder competition from nearby plants. During hot, dry days of August, the leaves act as bowls and gutters to catch and direct any falling water to the plant's crowns and roots.

As if that weren't enough, dandelions have bad breath. They exhale ethylene gas which sickens and hinders the growth of neighbors. Dandelions have been reported from fields and mowed areas as well as along roadways and paths on most of the islands. It is only necessary to look around a bit to find dandelions.

Verbascum thapsus L.   Common mullein.   *A*, Habit— × 0.5;   *B*, flowers— × 2;
C, capsules— × 2;   *D*, seeds— × 12.5.

MULLEIN
Verbascum thapsus L.

Common names: candlewick, torches, flannel leaf, Jacob's rod, cow's lungwort

Description:

Family:	SCROPHULARIACEAE (Figwort Family).
Source:	Naturalized from Eurasia.
Duration:	Biennial.
Habitat:	Poor dry and gravelly soil, highly disturbed areas.
Habit:	Rosette first year; stems erect; stout; sometimes branched near top; 1–8 feet tall; wooly throughout.
Leaves:	Rosette 8–24 inches in diameter, leaves 6–18 inches long, simple, entire, oblong, densely wooly; upper leaves alternate, simple, entire, wooly, bases enclosing stem to next leaf below giving stem a 4-winged appearance.
Flowers:	Yellow; 5 petals; ¾–1¼ inches in diameter; in long, dense, cylindrical spikes at top ends of stems. Blossoms June to September.
Reproduces:	By seeds.

Plants such as mullein have developed a great variety of ways to protect themselves from hazards of the environment. Purslane, for instance, has succulent tissue capable of storing enough water to see the plant through dry times. Great numbers of seeds capable of remaining viable for many years are produced by plants like amaranth and lambsquarters. Burdock insures wide distribution by means of hitch-hiking fruit while dandelion and milkweed do the same with windborne seeds. Plants like dandelion and milkweed further insure their perpetuation by being able to reproduce vegetatively from the roots. Sorrel and jewelweed throw their seeds forcefully out of the parent plant's immediate vicinity, thus cutting down on nearby competition from their offspring.

Plants protect themselves from animal and insect predators by disagreeable odors and unpleasant flavors, thorns, bristles, and tricky floral mechanisms like those of toadflax.

Mullein covers itself with a thick mat of interlacing hairs which serve as a sunshade to protect it from the heat and to keep it from losing too much water to the summer sun. The hairy covering also acts as a winter overcoat. So protected, mullein thrives well in exposed situations which it seems to favor. We would do well to look for it there.

Mullein has been seen . . .

   . . . in the open field just beyond the pergola on Gallops Island and is prominent in other fields and clearings on the island.

   . . . in the gun emplacements on Lovells Island.

   . . . in the field to the south of the wharf on Georges Island.

   . . . in the kettle hole on Thompson's Island.

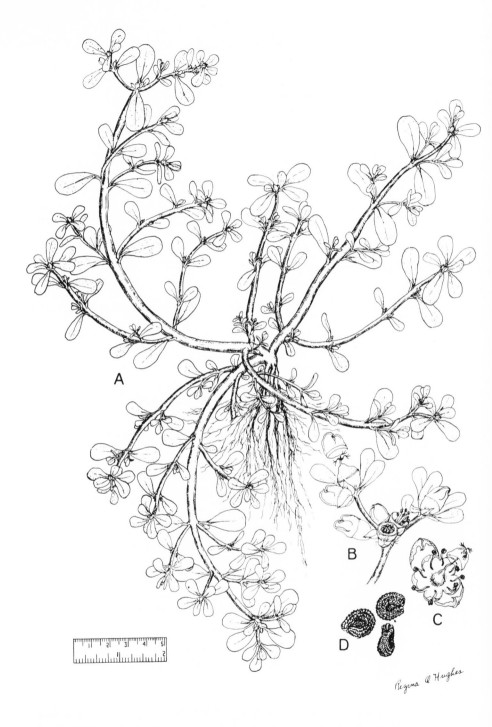

Portulaca oleracea L.   Common purslane.   *A*, Habit— × 0.5;   *B*, flowers and capsules— × 1.5;   *C*, flower open— × 4;   *D*, seeds— × 18.

PURSLANE

Portulaca oleracea L.

Common names: pusley, pigweed, duckweed, porcelain, portulaca

Description: Family: PORTULACACEAE (Purslane Family).

Source: Naturalized from Europe.

Duration: Annual.

Habitat: Cultivated fields and newly disturbed places.

Habit: Stems prostrate; much branched; forming mats; smooth; succulent; reddish-purple.

Leaves: Alternate (sometimes nearly opposite); simple; entire; sessile; wedge-shaped; thick; succulent; olive-green; in clusters at ends of branches.

Flowers: Yellow; 5 petals; ¼–½ inch in diameter; sessile; solitary in leaf axils. Blossoms June to November.

Fruit: Urn-shaped capsule opening at top by means of round lid; tiny.

Reproduces: By seeds.

When purslane's blossoms have gone, tiny urn-shaped capsules remain. The capsules open by means of round lids and the seeds spill out and scatter at the slightest disturbance. A single plant might produce as many as 190,000 seeds.

For sheer aggressiveness few weeds of cultivated areas will beat purslane. The seedlings, however, do not usually appear until the weather is very warm and the seeds rarely germinate unless the ground has been recently disturbed.

Purslane does well in rich garden soil in spite of competition from plants like amaranth and lambsquarters. Purslane is a low-grower and simply fills the ground beneath the competition. It does not do well where it must compete with plantain, mullein, and daisies, but purslane does appear from time to time in places where conditions are not particularly favorable.

It is a persistent weed in cultivated areas and has been known to set seed even after being pulled up and tossed aside. The scattered seeds are capable of remaining in the ground for many years, germinating only when favorable conditions prevail.

It takes a little scratching around to start purslane growing, and new plants might be discovered just about anywhere island fields have been recently disturbed.

Purslane was seen . . .

. . . near the picnic tables on Gallops Island after some earth was disturbed there in 1980. The plants were allowed to go to seed and purslane should grow there again someday . . . if it isn't doing so right now.

Oxalis stricta L.　Common yellow woodsorrel.　*A,* Habit— × 0.5;　*B,* leaves enlarged— × 1.25;　*C,* flower diagrams— × 2.5;　*D,* capsule— × 1.5;　*E,* seeds— × 10.

WOOD SORREL
Oxalis stricta L.

Common names: sour grass, ladies' sorrel, toad sorrel, pickle grass, sheep poison

Description: Family: OXALIDACEAE (Wood Sorrel Family).

Source: Native to the United States.

Duration: Perennial.

Habitat: Dry open soil.

Habit: Stems erect, up to 10 inches tall.

Leaves: Alternate; compound, with 3 pale-green, heart-shaped leaflets (clover-like); long-petioled.

Flowers: Yellow; 5 petals; ¼–½ inch diameter; sometimes red at base. Blossoms May to October.

Fruit: Slender seedpod; ½–1 inch long; 5-ridged; hairy; short-pointed beak.

Reproduces: By seeds.

Leaves of the yellow wood sorrel are sensitive to light, temperature, and moisture. The leaflets sometimes droop together in bright sunlight, at night, and in stormy weather. This has suggested various things to observers. Some have said the plants "sleep." Others have interpreted the movements as preventing injury to the plant from frost, since the folded position diminishes radiation; or that the formation of dew is prevented and the plant can begin transpiration promptly in the morning.

There are authorities who have still other points of view and if the attempts to explain this "sleep" phenomenon do nothing else, they give us at least an intriguing glimpse of one sort of problem with which some botanists grapple every day.

Oxalis stricta is slightly different from another yellow wood sorrel found on the islands . . . *Oxalis europaea* Jord. The most noticeable difference is the way in which the seedpods relate to their pedicels. In *Oxalis europaea* the pedicels and their seedpods both grow upward. The seedpods of *Oxalis stricta* also grow upward, but the pedicels turn downward from the stems (are deflexed), thus creating sharp angles as the illustration shows.

Wood sorrel is another of the "retiring" plants and you're on your own when it comes to finding it. It has been seen . . .
    . . . along the trails at the easterly end of Gallops Island.
    . . . between the edge-markers along the pathway to the reserved picnic area on Georges Island.
    . . . by the dead elms along the dirt roadway which crosses Thompson's Island at the south end of the old skating pond.

Stellaria media (L.) Vill.   Common chickweed.   *A*, Habit— × 0.5;   *B*, flower— × 3;
C, capsule— × 3.5;   *D*, seeds— × 7.5.

CHICKWEED

Stellaria media (L.) Vill.

Common names: bird seed, tongue grass, satin flower, flewort, palsywort

Description:	Family:	CARYOPHYLLACEAE (Pink Family).
	Source:	Naturalized from Eurasia.
	Duration:	Annual.
	Habitat:	Cultivated fields, gardens, grassy areas.
	Habit:	Stems low (trailing or ascending); up to 2½ feet; much branched; small hairs in lines; rooting at nodes.
	Leaves:	Opposite; simple; entire; ovate; ½ – 1¼ inches long; lower leaves petioled, oval, sometimes hairy; upper leaves sessile, smooth.
	Flowers:	White; 5 two-parted petals; pediceled; solitary from leaf axils or in loose clusters at ends of stems. Blossoms February to December (sometimes all winter).
	Reproduces:	By seeds or from creeping stems rooting at nodes.

Chickweed has more than a fair share of characteristics which make it one of our most successful common weeds. First of all, as anyone who searches for the plant on the islands will discover, chickweed is not particularly conspicuous. It is a low-grower, a plant of delicate features, and one which manages to lose itself in the company of more visible plants.

Accompanying the low-growing habit is an ability of the plant to root from the nodes of running stems. Once chickweed gets started, ordinary pulling is hardly enough to get rid of it. The plant simply breaks off at a rooted node and goes on growing unless every single rooted place is discovered and disposed of.

The name "winterweed" is a clue to another of its successful-weed attributes. Chickweed can endure much of what our winters have to offer and go on blossoming right through the season. Of course the blossoms are followed by seeds . . . between 2,500 and 15,000 per plant . . . which, according to one ambitious author, amounts to a potential annual production for a single chickweed plant of about 15,000 million brand new plants. That should be enough to make it easy to understand why one gardener suggested burning it out of the lawn with ammonium sulphate. The grass might burn also, but it would grow back, he said. One can't help wondering, though, about all those unburned seeds lurking just under the surface. After all, they are supposed to be tough enough to germinate after a run through a sparrow's digestive system and 90-days immersion in sea-water.

Several species of chickweed have been seen . . .
. . . in cellar holes on Gallops Island.
. . . spread out like a shawl of fine white lace over some tall grass in a thicket-trapped field on Lovells' north end.

Chrysanthemum Leucanthemum L. var. *prinnatifidum* Lecoq & Lamotte.   Field oxeye-
daisy.   *A,* Habit— × 0.5;   *B,* ray flower— × 2.5;   *C,* disc flower— × 2.5;
D, achenes— × 7.5;   *E,* involucral bracts- × 5.

DAISY
Chrysanthemum leucanthemum L.

Common names: ox-eye daisy, cow's eyes, love-me, farmer's curse, poverty weed

Description:

Family:	COMPOSITAE (Composite Family).	
Source:	Naturalized from Europe.	
Duration:	Perennial.	
Habitat:	Fields and fallow meadows, roadsides.	
Habit:	Stems erect; simple or branched toward the top; smooth; 1–3 feet tall.	
Leaves:	Basal leaves in rosette simple, long-petioled, and irregularly toothed; upper leaves on stem alternate, simple, sessile, narrow, toothed, and smooth-surfaced.	
Flowers:	20–30 white rays surrounding a yellow disk; 1¼–2 inches in diameter. Blossoms June to November.	
Reproduces:	By seeds and short rootstocks.	

That blossoms of plants within a given family often resemble one another is reflected by similarities in the names by which different members of the family are sometimes known. The name "daisy," for example, is not limited to a single member of the Composite Family. Blossoms of daisies, black-eyed susans, and fleabanes . . . all composites . . . are characterized by prominent centers surrounded by showy petals. And each has acquired "daisy" as one of its common names.

To help differentiate one from another in writing or conversation, a qualifying word is usually used as a part of the name. Thus we have ox-eye daisy or field-daisy for *Chrysanthemum leucanthemum*, yellow-daisy for black-eyed susan *(Rudbeckia hirta)*, and daisy fleabane for *Erigeron annuus.* Mayweed *(Anthemis cotula)*, another member of the family on the islands, is sometimes called "stinking-daisy" to help set it apart from family members which resemble it. It is also called "horse-daisy," "dog-daisy," pigsty-daisy," and "poison-daisy."

Even though the center may not appear, at a glance, to be particularly prominent, family members may still aspire to be called daisies. We have "blue-daisy" for chicory *(Cichorium intybus)*, "Irish-daisy" for dandelion *(Taraxacum officinale)*, and we sometimes run across "deadmen's-daisies" for the tiny blossoms of yarrow *(Achillea millefolium)*.

Even outside the family there are daisies. The common buttercup of the islands is known as the "butter-daisy" *(Ranunculus acris)*.

As lovers of sunny fields, ox-eye-daisies have been seen . . .
. . . in the field beyond the pergola on Gallops Island.
. . . just inside the gate to Fort Warren on Georges Island.
. . . in the gun emplacements on Lovells Island.
. . . in the large field at the north end of Thompson's Island.

Datura stramonium L.   Jimsonweed.   *A*, Habit, upper part of plant— × 0.5;   *B*, cauline
leaf— × 0.5;   *C*, ripe capsule— × 0.5;   *D*, seeds— × 3.

JIMSONWEED
Datura stramonium L.

Common names: thorn-apple, Devil's trumpet, stinkweed, fire-weed, madapple

Description:	Family:	SOLANACEAE (Nightshade Family).
	Source:	Naturalized from Asia.
	Duration:	Annual.
	Habitat:	Storm berms of beaches, rich gravelly soil.
	Habit:	Stems erect; stout; smooth; green; spreading branches in upper part; 1–5 feet.
	Leaves:	Alternate; simple; widely toothed; oval or triangular; smooth; sharp-pointed; 3–8 inches long; stout petioles; dark green; strongly scented.
	Flowers:	White to pinkish; trumpet-shaped (like wild petunia); 5-toothed border; 3–5 inches long; on short peduncles in axils of branches. Blossoms July to October.
	Fruit:	Egg-shaped capsule; prickly; 1½–3″long, 1″ diameter; downward turned papery disk at base.
	Reproduces:	By seeds.
	Other:	Foul-smelling; all parts dangerously poisonous.

It is enough to say, for some plants, that they are poisonous to eat. For others, and jimsonweed is one of them, an all-inclusive warning is most sensible. About the only way one can be sure of enjoying the plant without risk is to stand back and look at it.

For starters, it can be dangerous to touch, dangerous to smell, dangerous to eat, dangerous to make tea from, and dangerous to smoke. All of them have been tried . . . sometimes with fatal results. Although it was named Jamestown-weed (later reduced to jimsonweed) after some English soldiers from the colony at Jamestown had spent a few very uncomfortable days as a result of eating sprouts from the plant, children seem to have been its most frequent victims. They have sucked nectar from its blossoms, made tea from its leaves, and nibbled its seeds and fruits all with disastrous results. An Arnold Arboretum publication (see references) says that approximately one ounce of any part of the plant constitutes a lethal dose for a child.

Dust from the seeds has been known to cause persistent dilation of pupils of the eyes (known as "corn-picker's eye"), as has rubbing the eyes after handling the plant. Susceptible individuals may suffer dermatitis after contact with the leaves, flowers, or fruits.

It has been seen . . .

. . . along the sea wall to the left of the pergola on Gallops Island.
. . . on the beaches around Ram's Head on Lovells Island.
. . . on higher ground at the site of the original farmhouse of Thompson's.

Habit for all— × 0.5.   *A, Plantago lanceolata* L.   Buckhorn plantain.   *a,* Flower—
× 2.5;   *b,* capsule— × 3; *c,* seed— × 5.   B, Plantago major L. Broadleaf plantain.
a, Flower— × 2.5;   *b,* capsule— × 3; *c,* seeds— × 5.   C,*Plantago rugelii* Decne.
Blackseed plantain.   *a,* Flower— × 2.5;   *b,* capsule— × 2.5;   *c,* seeds— × 3.

PLANTAIN

Plantago major L.

Common names: whiteman's foot, waybroad, snakeweed, healing blade, bird seed

Description: Family: PLANTAGINACEAE (Plantain Family).

Source: Naturalized from Europe.

Duration: Perennial.

Habitat: Along roadsides and in trails and pathways.

Habit: Stems erect; slender; leafless; smooth or hairy; ending in long spike with blunt end.

Leaves: In basal rosettes; simple; entire; oval; long-petioled; prominently veined.

Flowers: White or pale-green; tiny; appear irregularly in spike at end of stem. Blossoms June to October.

Reproduces: By seeds and new shoots from roots.

The several species of plantain on the islands can be divided into those with broad leaves and long spikes and those with narrow leaves and short spikes.

The broad-leaved one which concerns us here *(Plantago major),* is much like another *(Plantago rugelii* Dcne.*)* in that both have leaves with oval blades which are prominently veined, have long petioles, and look like large, flattened spoons. Subtle differences like leaf thickness, hairiness, or a redness in the petioles of *P. rugelii* help botanists tell the difference when necessary. The tall flower spikes are also similar, but on looking closely it will be seen that those of the purple-stemmed plantain are narrower, more tapered, and end in a point while those of the broad-leaved plantain *(P. major)* are blunt at the ends as the illustration shows.

If any examples are needed to demonstrate the toughness of plantain, there are probably none better than specimens to be found growing in the heavily traveled pathways on most of the islands. They certainly do not become the largest and lushest of plants, but like most weeds they do persist and they do survive in adverse circumstances, even to the extent that they will send up diminutive flower stalks, set seed, and continue to spread themselves around.

Plantain has been seen . . .

. . . in small chip-covered clearings that are scattered here and there on Gallops Island.

. . . in places like the sheltered grassy depression which runs along behind the gun emplacements on Lovells Island.

. . . in tall grass at the edge of the trail as it runs through the sumac north of the athletic field on Thompson's Island.

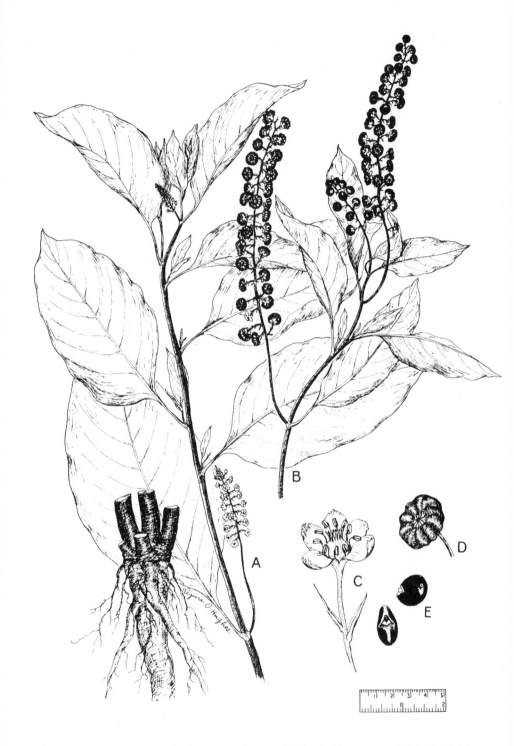

Phytolacca americana L.   Pokeweed.   *A,* Habit, in flower— × 0.5;   *B,* fruiting raceme— × 0.5;   *C,* flower— × 5;   *D,* berry— × 2;   *E,* seeds— × 2.5.

POKE

Phytolacca americana L.

Common names: garget, pigeon berry, red-ink berry, pocan bush, dyer's weed

Description: Family: PHYTOLACCACEAE (Pokeweed Family).

             Source: Native to the United States.

             Duration: Perennial.

             Habitat: Rich ground, recent clearings.

             Habit: Stems erect; stout; hollow; smooth; branched in upper portions; 4–12 feet tall; green at first, turning red-purple as plant matures.

             Leaves: Alternate; simple; oblong; entire; 4–12 inches long; smooth; sharp-pointed; long-petioled.

             Flowers: White or pinkish; ¼ inch diameter; in long racemes at ends of branches and opposite the leaves in upper part of plant. Blossoms July to October.

             Fruit: Dark purple berry with staining red juice.

             Reproduces: By seeds.

             Other: Roots, seeds, mature plant poisonous to eat. Berries questionable.

Though the young green shoots of poke are favored as spring potherbs in some places, the root is always poisonous to eat and once the plant begins to mature and turn red, the above ground parts become unsafe to eat. The berries are said to have been used to make tarts and pies, but the absence of recipes suggests this may be more an exception than a rule and wise persons heed the cautions of authorities and avoid the berries as food in any form. There are records of seed-poisoning.

For a plant so striking in its maturity, poke can be surprisingly inconspicuous. Newly sprung from seed, it is delicate and does not resemble the stout spring shoots sent up by well established roots. The older plants have a way of settling in sheltered and shadowed places where branching forms, leaf greens, flower creams, stem and berry reds play hide and seek in changing light.

Such is the case for the old poke plants which have captured places for themselves at the base of the hill where open woods give way to storm berms at the northeastern end of Thompson's Island. But mature plants do appear in the open as well and can be found in the kettle hole along the Southwest Trail.

Look for the plants in clearings in island woods and in waste places where the soil is rich and gravelly.

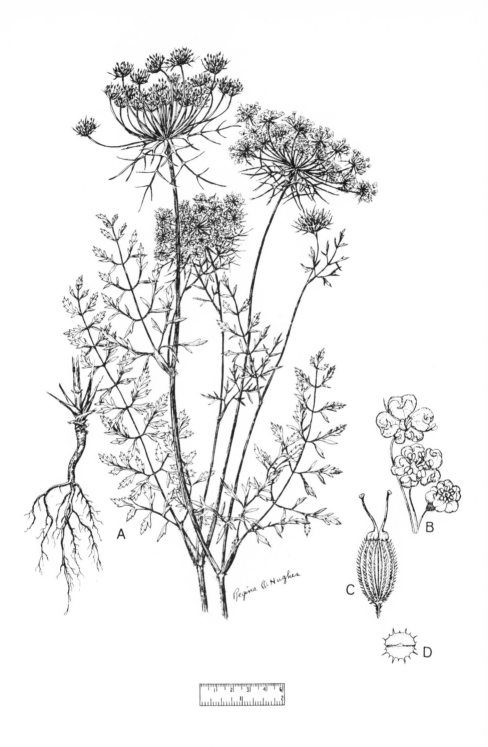

Daucus carota L.   Wild carrot.   *A*, Habit— × 0.5;   *B*, flowers— × 5;   *C*, schizocarp—
× 5;   *D*, cross section of fruit, showing 2 mericarps— × 3.

QUEEN ANNE'S LACE
Daucus carota L.

Common names: wild carrot, bird's nest, lace flower, Devil's plague, fiddle

Description: Family: UMBELLIFERAE (Parsley Family).

Source: Naturalized from Europe.

Duration: Biennial.

Habitat: Old meadows, roadsides, sunny fields.

Habit: During its first year the plant produces only a basal rosette of leaves which anyone familiar with carrot leaves will recognize without difficulty. In its second year the plant produces stems which are erect, slender, tough, branching, covered with bristly hair, and up to 3-feet tall.

Leaves: Leaves alternate, decompound (carrotlike); basal leaves long-petioled; stem leaves sessile, clasping, and smaller than basal leaves.

Flowers: White; in dense, compound umbels at ends of stems. Umbels usually 3–4″ across but may sometimes reach 6″. Umbels look like white lace when viewed from above. Blossoms May to October.

Reproduces: By seeds.

Other: Scraped root smells like carrot.

The fact that gardeners are advised to place brush amongst the flower-bed Queen Anne's lace to protect it against the wind should make all other differences superfluous in insuring that our wild Queen Anne's lace *(Daucus carota)* is not to be confused with *Trachymene caerulea,* a plant of flower gardens, which also carries the name Queen Anne's lace. Wild Queen Anne will not yield easily to the wind any more than it will yield easily to much of anything else. Besides, it has no blue-blossom counterpart and does not smell as nice as the domestic Queen Anne.

It certainly was no delicate thing John Burroughs had in mind when he wrote that if a farmer cut off the head of Queen Anne he would, within a week, have five staring at him which, if treated in like manner, would be replaced apace by ten. Queen Anne, it seems is more Hydra than Hydra herself.

All of this helps to explain, perhaps, why Muenscher says that wild carrots cause more trouble in meadows after the hay has been removed and that second crops from the same fields may consist of more wild carrots than grass or clover.

Queen Anne has been seen . . .

. . . in clearings by ruins of the cement-block foundations on the hillside just above the pergola on Gallops Island.

. . . in gun emplacements and surrounding fields on Lovells Island.

. . . inside the gate to Fort Warren and south of the wharf on Georges Island.

. . . on the large open slope at the northeastern end of Thompson's Island.

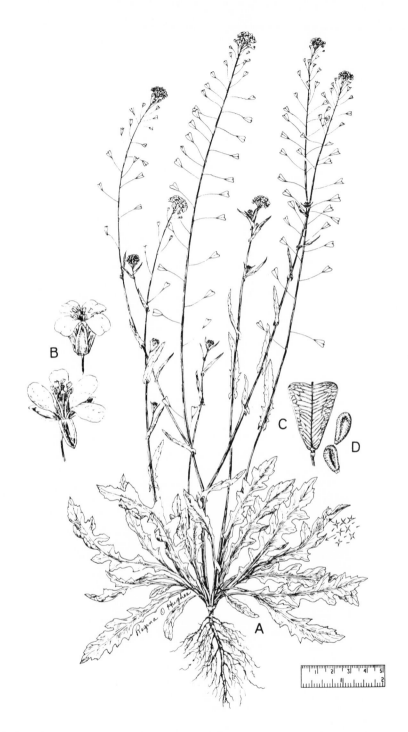

Capsella bursa-pastoris (L.) Medic.   Shepherdspurse.   *A*, Habit— × 0.5;   *B*, flowers—
× 5;   *C*, silicle— × 4;   *D*, seeds— × 10.

SHEPHERD'S PURSE
Capsella bursa-pastoris (L.) Medic.

Common names: clappedepouch, casewort, mother's heart, toyweed, St. James' weed

Description: Family: CRUCIFERAE (Mustard Family).

Source: Naturalized from Europe.

Duration: Annual.

Habitat: Gardens, lawns, wasteplaces.

Habit: Stem erect; branched; 4–24 inches tall; wiry.

Leaves: Alternate (rosette at base); simple; toothed or lobed; 2–4 inches long; stem leaves few, sessile, arrow-shaped, and smaller than basal leaves.

Flowers: White; 4-petalled; tiny; in elongated racemes at ends of branches; pedicels slender. Blossoms March to December.

Fruit: Triangular (heart-shaped) seed pods; appx. ¼ inch long.

Reproduces: By seeds.

Shepherd's purse is one of our commonest weeds, but its small size and wiry form make it so difficult to see that it may not seem as common as it really is. The plant is common enough, though, to be regularly listed in writings about wild foods, a listing which may be encouraged by the fact that shepherd's purse can be found blooming from early spring into the snows of winter, will survive flooding, drought, freezing, and produces seeds which will sprout after lying dormant in the earth for 35 years.

The inconspicuous specimens usually found on the islands make it hard to believe that the plant could ever serve as a market crop, yet in the early 1800's at least two British writers reported that the plants were sold in Philadelphia markets. Others, including at least one who lived near Philadelphia, were inclined to discount the reports and preferred to call shepherd's purse a "worthless little intruder from Europe," thereby fuelling a smoldering controversy which never seems to have burst into flame. The accuracy of those old reports is still questioned publicly from time to time and it is worth noting that leaves of this highly variable weed have been credited with at least 63 different forms and some of them might well have been of market quality.

Shepherd's purse has been seen . . .
. . . along the sea wall south of the wharf on Georges Island.
. . . by the steps in front of the administration building on Thompson's Island.

Achillea millefolium L.   Common yarrow.   *A*, Habit— × 0.5;   *B*, enlarged leaves and stem— × 5;   *C*, flower head— × 4;   *D*, female and male flowers— × 5;   *E*, seeds— × 6.

YARROW

Achillea millefolium L.

Common names: nosebleed, carpenter's weed, soldier's woundwort, milfoil, thousand-seal

Description:

Family:	COMPOSITAE (Composite Family).	
Source:	Naturalized from Europe.	
Duration:	Perennial.	
Habitat:	Exposed sunny fields and along roadsides.	
Habit:	Stems erect; angular; rough; occasionally branched; 6–40 inches high.	
Leaves:	Alternate; bipinnately divided; 2–6 inches long; sometimes mistaken for ferns during first year when flower-stalks and flowers are not present; strong odor when crushed.	
Flowers:	Yellow centers surrounded by 4–6 (usually 5) white or pink petal-like rays; in dense, flat-topped corymbs after first year; tiny. Blossoms June to November.	
Reproduces:	By seeds and rootstocks.	

Because yarrow's spreading rootstocks keep it growing in spite of repeated mowings, because the plant will tolerate the tread of many feet, because it can remain green in times of drought long after other greens have yellowed and become brown, yarrow was one of the plants included in a mixture designed to carpet cemeteries all over Europe following the First World War.

Before that, the plant's rich color and velvety texture were welcomed in the meadow-like medieval lawns which garden-boys worked to keep free of an undesirable weed we now know as grass. One of yesterday's valued lawn plants has become one of today's most common weeds.

It should not be too difficult to find this plant in almost any open field or mowed area on the islands. Certainly the insects have no trouble finding yarrow. One observer counted more than 120 different species of bees and butterflies visiting a single yarrow plant in one day.

Yarrow has been seen . . .
   . . . in the large flat clearing atop Gallops Island.
   . . . in the gun emplacements on Lovells Island.
   . . . in the overgrown fields at the south end of Georges Island.
   . . . on the east-facing slope by the track on Thompson's Island.

Polygonum persicaria L.   Ladysthumb.   *A,* Habit— × 0.5;   *B,* spike— × 3;
C, ocrea— × 1.5;   *D,* achenes— × 5.

LADY'S THUMB

Polygonum persicaria L.

Common names: knotweed, red-knees, red-shanks, heart's-ease, lover's-pride

Description: Family: POLYGONACEAE (Buckwheat Family).

Source: Naturalized from Europe.

Duration: Annual.

Habitat: Cultivated ground, roadsides.

Habit: Stems ascending or decumbent; smooth; jointed; swollen at nodes; reddish above nodes.

Leaves: Alternate; simple; entire; lanceolate; 1–6 inches long; ¼–1¼ inches wide; petioles red; ocrea bristly; purplish or gray triangular spot near center of blade.

Flowers: Pink; tiny; in dense, erect spikes from the sheathed nodes. Blossoms June to October.

Reproduces: By seeds.

It is necessary to look closely at four knotweeds found on the islands if the plants are to be recognized as all belonging to the Buckwheat Family. Unlike the plants of different genuses which are called "daisy" because of similarities in appearance, these four plants don't look much alike even though they share "knotweed" as a common name and are more closely related than the daisies in that they all belong to the same genus, *Polygonum*.

Polygonum aviculare L. (prostrate knotweed) is usually a ground-hugger with small leaves. *Polygonum persicaria* (Lady's thumb) has larger leaves and is a much coarser plant with a tendency to grow upright. *Polygonum convolvulus* L. (black bindweed) is so unlike other members of the genus in leaf form and its twining, vine-like habit that some people are more inclined to identify the plant with morning glory than with knotweed. And *Polygonum cuspidatum* Sieb. and Zucc. (Japanese knotweed) is a giant among them. The plants grow eight or nine feet tall, have saucer-size leaves, and stems thick as broomsticks which resemble bamboo.

But careful examination will show that they all have the knobby joints with tubelike sheaths (ocreae) so characteristic of the members of the genus *Polygonum*.

Lady's thumb has been seen . . .

   . . . along the walks by the cement-block foundation remnants just uphill from the solar facility on Gallops Island.

   . . . in the large field east of the track on Thompson's Island.

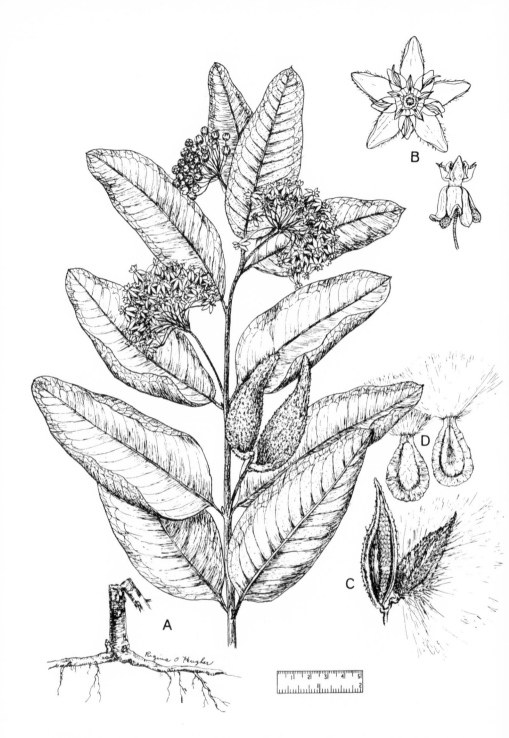

Asclepias syriaca L.   Common milkweed.   *A*, Habit— × 0.5;   *B*, flower, upper view— × 3.5: side view— × 2;   *C*, follicles— × 0.5;   *D*, seeds with coma— × 3.

MILKWEED

Asclepias syriaca L.

Common names: silkweed, swallow-wort, antelope horn, rubber tree, wild cotton

Description:

	Family:	ASCLEPIADACEAE (Milkweed Family).
	Source:	Native to the United States.
	Duration:	Perennial.
	Habitat:	Dry fields, pastures, roadsides, thickets.
	Habit:	Stems erect; unbranched; covered with fine hairs; 3–5 feet tall.
	Leaves:	Opposite (sometimes whorled); simple; entire; thick; oblong; rounded at ends; 4–10 inches long, 1½–5 inches wide; undersides prominently veined and downy; upper surfaces smooth.
	Flowers:	Pink to white; 5-petalled; in ball-like umbels at tips of stems and in axils of upper leaves; sweet-smelling. Blossoms June to August.
	Fruit:	Hairy, horn-shaped pod; covered with soft, spine-like projections; 3–7 inches long; pedicel recurved.
	Reproduces:	By seeds and rootstocks.
	Other:	All parts of plant ooze thick milky sap when broken.

Because milkweed produces new plants from rootstocks as well as from seed, it is often found growing in patches. Pulling the plants up rarely injures the root system since they simply break off where they are attached. The roots remain undisturbed and go on spreading and producing new shoots. The separation can be easily demonstrated by firmly grasping a milkweed stalk at the base and pulling straight up with a steady, even force. In most cases the plant will come out free, clean, white, and rootless.

The roots, running along 6–30 inches underground are usually well below surface disturbances and regular cultivation rarely clears a field of milkweed. The plants defy the farmer's plow and naturalist John Burroughs toyed with the idea that the blade must have taught the roots to run so deep. "What other enemy or circumstance could have so driven them into the ground?" He dropped the idea, though, with the thought that deep growth was doubtless much older than the plow.

Milkweed has been seen . . .
. . . in the large field atop Gallops Island.
. . . in the fields in front of the gun emplacements on Lovells Island.
. . . in the dry moat on Georges Island.
. . . in the kettle hole on Thompson's Island.

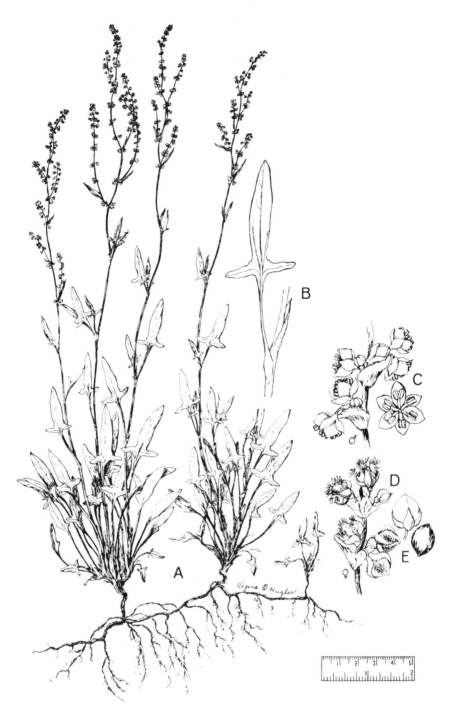

Rumex acetosella L. Red sorrel. *A*, Habit— × 0.5; *B*, leaf detail— × 1.5;
C, Staminate flowers— × 7.5; *D*, pistillate flowers— × 7.5; *E*, achenes, in and out of
calyx— × 10.

SHEEP SORREL

Rumex acetosella L.

Common names: little vinegar-plant, sour grass, toad sorrel, cuckoo meat, gentlemen's sorrel

Description: Family: POLYGONACEAE (Buckwheat Family).

Source: Naturalized from Eurasia.

Duration: Perennial.

Habitat: Worn-out fields, sour soil.

Habit: Stems erect; slender; low, 6–8 inches high; branched at top.

Leaves: Alternate; simple; entire; smooth; rosette in early growth; lower leaves arrow-shaped; upper leaves lanceolate or linear.

Flowers: Reddish to pink; tiny; in close panicles at ends of stems. Blossoms June to October.

Reproduces: By seeds and creeping roots.

That certain plants may be poisonous in some ways to some people and not poisonous to others, poisonous under some conditions and not poisonous under others, is worth knowing. As a case in point, sheep sorrel is sometimes included in lists of poisonous plants because it is reported to cause dermatitis in susceptible persons. It is also listed as a plant which may be poisonous to eat in large quantities because of oxalates it might contain. Usually added, is information that "nibblings" are quite safe and that cooking seems to render the plants harmless. Spinach is on the same list.

When dealing with wild plants it is good to know which are poisonous and which are not. It is also good to know something about what is meant when a plant is said to be poisonous and whether it is reported as poisonous to humans or simply to animals.

There are plants like poison ivy which are poisonous to contact; some, like jimsonweed, which are poisonous to sniff; and others, like poison hemlock, which are poisonous to eat. In some cases, as in all of the examples used here, the plants may be considered poisonous for more than one reason.

The subject obviously calls for close attention and books by Muenscher and Kingsbury, listed in the references, are good places to begin.

Sheep sorrel has been seen . . .

. . . on the pathway leading toward Hull from the top of the hill on Gallop's Island.

. . . on the path between the wharf and the reserved picnic area on Georges Island.

. . . along the Northeast Trail beyond the track on Thompson's Island.

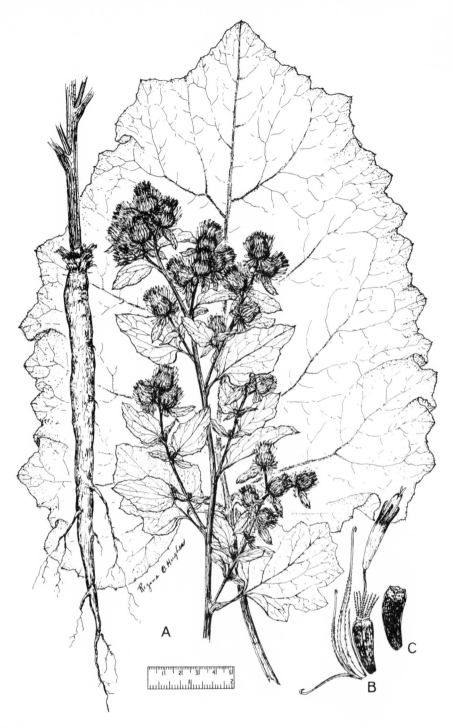

Arctium minus Bernh.   Common burdock.   *A,* Habit: root, leaf, upper raceme of
heads— × 0.5;   *B,* flower and phyllaries— × 4;   *C,* achene— × 3.

BURDOCK

Arctium minus Bernh.

Common names: beggar's buttons, clotbur, bardana, jealous woman, personata

Description: Family: COMPOSITAE (Composite Family).

Source: Naturalized from Europe.

Duration: Biennial.

Habitat: Neglected farmlands, rich soil

Habit: Stems erect; coarse; branching 3–5 feet tall. Produces only a rosette of large basal leaves during first year.

Leaves: Alternate; simple; entire; undersides of large basal leaves covered with a thick mat of short hairs which gives them a soft gray color; dull pale green on top; heart-shaped with long petioles which are u-shaped in cross-section; upper leaves smaller, ovate, and without the heavy mat of hair on their undersides.

Flowers: Purple; resemble those of thistles but are not so large; ½–¾ inches in diameter; sessile or on short peduncles; single or in raceme-like clusters in leaf axils. Blossoms July to October.

Reproduces: By seeds.

Burdock makes an ideal dreamer's plant. Luther Burbank thought enough about its possibilities to experiment with it himself and he believed that anyone aware how much some of our garden vegetables have been improved through cultivation would recognize burdock's possibilities immediately. Because the plant is palatable when growing wild and has no poisonous principle, it is an experimenter's dream to Burbank's way of thinking. His recommendation was to strive for an improved root and a reduced bitterness.

Others have been interested enough in the plant to establish burdock plantations and Mrs. M. Grieve figured that a single acre of burdock would yield 1500–2000 pounds of dried root. A retail market value of $1.50–$3.00 per pound was placed on the product in 1978 by an author involved with collecting and marketing wild plants. The dreamer putting those figures together will come up with a dollar yield somewhere between $2,500–$6,000 to the acre.

It makes for pleasant speculation on a hot summer afternoon to watch that pesky weed grow all by itself and know that a single plant may produce 400,000 seeds, enough to cover the whole of Gallops Island . . . planted and thinned as the experts say. For the dreamer, that much burdock would amount to about $84,000, give or take . . .

Burdock has been seen . . .
   . . . in the field on the south end of Georges Island.
   . . . on the hill behind the ordnance storehouse on Lovells Island.
   . . . on the east-sloping hillside beside the gym on Thompson's Island.

Cichorium intybus L.   Chicory.   *A*, Habit— × 0.5;   *B*, terminal portion of inflorescence;
C, involucre— × 2.5;   *D*, flower— × 2.5;   *E*, achenes— × 7.5.

CHICORY

Cichorium intybus L.

Common names: blue sailors, ragged sailors, coffee-weed, blue dandelion, waiter-by-the-way

Description:	Family:	COMPOSITAE (Composite Family).
	Source:	Naturalized from Europe.
	Duration:	Perennial.
	Habitat:	Lawns, roadsides, fencerows, sunny fields.
	Habit:	Stems erect; hollow; sparsely branched; stiff; rough-hairy; 1–8 feet tall; sometimes reddish.
	Leaves:	Those of basal rosette toothed (dandelion-like); long-petioled; 4–8″ long; smooth to rough-hairy. Upper leaves alternate; simple; entire or toothed; arrow-shaped and clasping; smaller than basal leaves.
	Flowers:	Blue; 1–3 per cluster in leaf axils or at the ends of short, stiff branches; 1–1¼″ in diameter; blossoms sometimes white or pink. Blossoms June to October.
	Reproduces:	By seeds and roots.
	Other:	Milky sap.

Chicory is usually thought of as an extender for coffee, but has long been enjoyed by some people as a beverage in its own right. There was a time when chicory coffee was so popular in Europe that there was not enough chicory to meet the demand and the beverage suffered the same fate as real coffee and ground chicory root began to include admixtures such as sawdust, roasted beans, and dried horse-liver.

At the end of the 19th century agricultural experts in this country saw a prosperous future for chicory if it were grown commercially in the United States. In the excitement of anticipation, it was estimated that a productive acre of land would grow 15-tons of roots and yield a price of $7.00 per ton at a cost of less than $40.00 for each acre. The prosperous future never materialized. Two decades into the 20th century the experts were less optimistic. William L. Nelson, U.S. Congressman from Missouri, writing for the Sears-Roebuck manual *Farm Knowledge* in 1919, said that chicory had not been much grown in this country due to uncertainty of manufacturing the crop into a finished product.

Today, though chicory is a farm crop in some places, it is more likely to be thought of as a roadside weed and, when talked about at all, is most often discussed in terms of ounces and pennies.

Chicory has been seen . . .

. . . in many fields and clearings on Gallops Island.

. . . in fields and along the edges of pathways on Lovells Island.

. . . in filled areas behind the water-taxi information booth on Georges Island.

. . . near the picnic tables by the wharf on Thompson's Island. In 1980 a plant with white blossoms grew along the east side of the gym.

Malva neglecta Wallr.   Common mallow.   *A*, Habit— × 0.5;   *B*, enlarged
branchlet— × 2;   *C*, flower diagram— × 5;   *D*, carpel— × 5;   *E*, seeds— × 5.

COMMON MALLOW
Malva neglecta Wallr.

Common names: cheeses, amours, malice, shirt-button plant, cuckoo's bread

Description: Family: MALVACEAE (Mallow Family).

Source: Naturalized from Europe.

Duration: Annual or biennial.

Habitat: New lawns, cultivated grounds, edges of gardens and walls.

Habit: Procumbent; pubescent; many-branched and spreading.

Leaves: Alternate; simple; round with heart-shaped base; scalloped and with 5–7 shallow lobes; up to size of 50-cent piece in diameter; long-petioled.

Flowers: White or pale-lilac; 5 petals (notched); ½–¾ inch in diameter; singly or in clusters in leaf axils; delicate. Blossoms April to October.

Fruit: Round; flat; hard; green; about ¼ inch in diameter; resemble tiny cheeses.

Reproduces: By seeds.

Although Job may have believed the need to eat leaves of mallow was a sign of destitution, there was a time when the plant was considered desirable enough for the Egyptians to cultivate it as a potherb. The Greeks and Romans once valued mallow as a food plant. Sturtevant says it was one of two plants grown by the Greeks at the temple of Apollo as a symbol of man's first nourishment.

Malva neglecta is supposed to have appeared in the New World before 1699 and has had plenty of time to become one of our most common weeds. But anyone searching for mallow on the islands may be more inclined to agree with those who see the plant as an innocuous one than to side with those who call it one of our most pernicious weeds. Were mallow truly a pernicious weed, one which causes great damage, we could expect its presence to be much more evident than it usually is. Those who say mallow can be found on cultivated ground, new lawns, farmyards, and waste places might just as well say that the plant can be found anywhere people are likely to be . . . if one looks hard.

Mallow has been seen . . .

. . . on Gallops Island in a little clearing at the west end of the pathway that begins just uphill from the solar facility.

. . . on Georges Island among the stones on the north side, close to where the boats come between it and Gallops Island.

GALLOPS ISLAND

1. Pergola.

2. The field just behind the pergola is an especially good hunting area. Once the season is well advanced, the easiest plants to see will be the taller ones like Queen Anne's lace, chicory, curly dock, and yarrow. There will be others down in the grass. Look for them.

   yarrow, mugwort, daisy, chicory, Queen Anne's lace, curly dock, mullein.

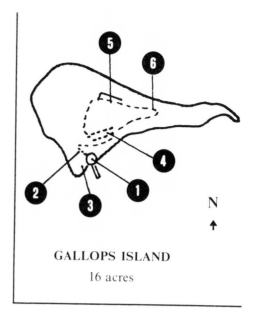

GALLOPS ISLAND

16 acres

N ↑

3. Around the seawall is a good spot for jimsonweed, but other interesting plants will be found there as well.

   jimsonweed.

4. The area of the cement-block foundations and old walkways is a "look-sharp" area. Much of it is shaded by trees and it is full of nooks and crannies that should be looked into. Check the far sides of any walls, all around their bases, and along the edges of walkways. There are scattered open spaces in this area and you will find it rewarding to check all of them carefully. Picnic tables will be found in the vicinity of the west end of the walkways. It is in this general area that you might find some amaranth or purslane. East from the walkways are some interesting cellar-holes in which chickweed and coltsfoot *(Tussilago farfara* L.*)* can sometimes be found. Open cellar-holes always seem to harbor some sort of interesting plant life.

   amaranth, lambsquarters, Queen Anne's lace, mallow, plantain, Lady's thumb, purslane, chickweed, coltsfoot.

5. At the top of the hill is a place with many more plants than are discussed in the book. It is a super place for the plant-hunter. Down the bank to the north of this area is where the poison-ivy-bound asparagus can be found.

   yarrow, mugwort, milkweed, poison ivy.

6. Along this east slope, look for: *wood sorrel, sheep sorrel.*

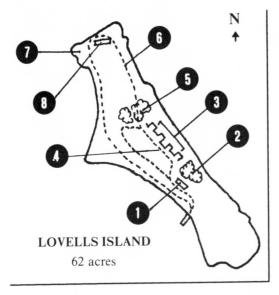

N
↑

LOVELLS ISLAND

1. Foundations of ordnance storehouse on right-hand side of old asphalt roadway mark a good place to start your climb to #2.

2. This hilltop grove has trees which ripen bucketfuls of tasty sour cherries early in July. It is a good place to eat lunch and examine some giant burdock along with a few catnip plants.

   burdock, catnip.

3. The gun emplacements, besides holding examples of many of the plants included in the book, also have a peach tree which produced nice fruit in 1980. There are many fruit trees on the islands. Watch for them.

   yarrow, mugwort, milkweed, daisy, curly dock, mullein.

4. The "trapped" walkway behind the gun emplacements is a good place to look for plants like plantain which seem to thrive in the cool, shaded environment.

   chicory, plantain, dandelion.

5. At the foot of the "highlands," is a veritable thicket with many plants yet to be discovered. It is here that one of the chickweeds can sometimes be seen lying in lace-like sheets over knee-high grass. It is the sort of area cattails might be expected, but I have yet to find them.

   poison ivy, chickweed.

6. Berms. Plenty of jimsonweed here and, if you are lucky, a lot of tumble mustard *(Sisymbrium altissimum* L.) for which see Levering, Peterson, or Newcomb.

7. Ram's Head.

8. Battery Tirrell.

GEORGES ISLAND

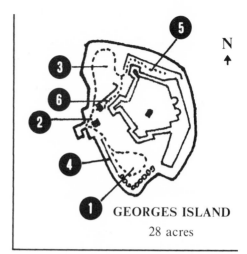

GEORGES ISLAND
28 acres

N ↑

1. This is what is referred to as the "south field," or "field toward Hull." It is an excellent place to look for specimens of the plants discussed.

   yarrow, burdock, mugwort, lambsquarters, Queen Anne's lace, curly dock, dandelion, mullein.

2. The area next to the large brick building near the wharf includes the walk toward the reserved picnic area as well as the water-taxi information booth. This is the place where anything growing is doing so under extremely difficult conditions. There are a lot of plants here but, as will be seen, they are not the most impressive examples. Alongside the path you may notice a plant which looks a bit like chickweed, but has scarlet blossoms. It will be the poorman's weatherglass . . . scarlet pimpernel . . . *(Anagallis arvensis L.).*

   lambsquarters, chicory, wood sorrel, sheep sorrel.

3. Reserved picnic area. At the edge of the rocks to the north, Mayweed often grows in quantity. Mallow has been seen at the edge of the beach to the west.

   mayweed, lambsquarters, mallow, plantain.

4. Several species of wild mustard grow along this seawall. Shepherd's purse has been found here in great quantity.

   shepherd's purse, plantain, dandelion.

5. After the south field, the dry moat is the best all-around plant hunting place on Georges Island. Among other unlisted plants, orange day lily *(Hemerocallis fulva* L.) and coltsfoot will be found growing there. Nesting pheasants have also been observed in the moat. If you are fortunate enough to discover a nest, do not disturb it.

   milkweed, dandelion, and others.

6. This is the area referred to as the "entrance to Fort Warren." Actually, it is a gate which leads into the dry moat and up to the ramp that goes through the walls into the parade ground. It is another good hunting area.

   daisy, Queen Anne's lace.

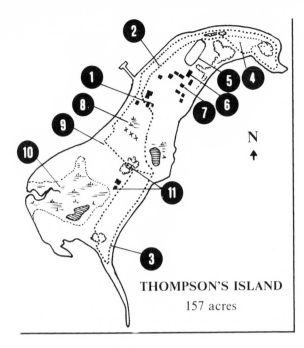

THOMPSON'S ISLAND

1. The Visitor Information Center. The place to stop for a brochure about Thompson's Island Trails and additional information about good plant-hunting locations. Once you leave the boat and are on your way to the Center, notice the beach and walkway areas around the end of the wharf. They are good hunting spots.

THOMPSON'S ISLAND

157 acres

N ↑

2. The Northeast Trail.
Lots of good plants along here. Watch along the edges, in the fields it crosses, and on the berms at the farthest turning point.
sheep sorrel, poke, dandelions, plantain, curly dock, mugwort, yarrow, daisies.

3. Southwest Trail. Equally as rewarding to the plant-hunter as the northeast trail.
sheep sorrel, cattail, wood sorrel, jimsonweed, milkweed, poke, mullein, and others.

4. Mentioned in the descriptions as the large field at the north end, this is a beautiful meadow with all of the trappings in summertime. The plants to be found here are *daisies, Queen Anne's lace, mullein,* and some of the others listed for the Northeast Trail.

5. The large field east of the track has a character which is quite different from that of the large meadow. Particularly interesting is the area along the edges of the woods to the north and east. It might be the perfect field to try an unpricked and unbloodied ramble through the brambles.
yarrow, Lady's thumb, dandelion.

6. A number of the plants find bays along the gym's east wall fine places to grow. It was here that the white chicory was seen in 1980.
chicory, dandelion, Queen Anne's lace, lambsquarters, burdock, plantain.

7. Administration Building.
    shepherd's purse.

8. Old skating pond and dead elms. When this area is dry, it is a good prowling place to find new growth of plants which don't grow there when it is wet. *cattails, sheep sorrel, wood sorrel.* Those who want a look at tansy can find its fern-like leaves along the cartway by the dead elms. In late summer they should be flagged by the golden blossoms, like rayless daisies.

9. The kettle hole. For a uniquely protected environment, the kettle hole is hard to beat. Take time to look into it. Compare the health of plants here with the same species you may have noticed elsewhere. It is also interesting to look for patterns in the distribution of the different kinds of plants in the kettle.

10. Saltmarsh. A study in itself. For more information, see the island brochure and read *Life and Death of the Saltmarsh* by John and Mildred Teal. In the fields of the slopes that rise toward the northeast from the marsh some good examples of *milkweed and mullein* are sometimes in evidence.

11. Original farmhouse and root-cellars.
    jimsonweed, day lily, mullein, butter and eggs, curly dock, burdock.

GLOSSARY

Achene	A small dry fruit with one seed and a thin outer covering which does not open or burst when ripe and dry. (See burdock, daisy, and mugwort illustrations.)
Alternate (leaves)	Growing along a stem singly, one leaf at a node, first on one side then on the other.
Anaphrodisiac	Something which lessens sexual desire.
Annual	A plant which lives a single growing season.
Ascending	Rising upwards at an angle.
Axil	Upper angle between leaf and stem.

Beak	Point or extension at end of seedpod.
Biennial	A plant which lives two growing seasons.
Bipinnate	Twice pinnate. Leaflets on main axis pinnate (feather-formed) and the leaflets themselves are pinnate.
Bract	A modified leaf, usually small, papery, and imperfectly developed. (See daisy illustration.)
Brambles	Prickly shrubs of the rose family, such as raspberry, blackberry, etc.

Capsule	A pod or fruit which contains seeds and usually bursts when ripe (see butter and eggs, jimsonweed, and wood sorrel).
Carpel	A part of the ovary which bears ovules, the female portion of the flower (see mallow illustration).
Cauline	Located on the stem (see jimsonweed illustration).
Caustic	Burning, being able to eat away or destroy tissue by chemical action.
Clasping	Leaf partly or completely surrounding stem.
Coma	A tuft of hairs at the end of a seed (see milkweed illustration).
Compound (leaf)	Made up of several distinct parts. Refers to a leaf made up of several leaflets, like clover and wood sorrel.
Copperas	Ferrous sulphate, a green, crystalline compound used in dyeing and the making of ink.

Corymb	A raceme with lower flower stalks longer than those above so that all flowers come to same level.
Counterirritant	An agent for producing irritation in one part of the body to counteract it in another part.

Decompound	Compounded more than once.
Decumbent	Lying flat, with the tip growing upward.
Deflexed	Bent or turned sharply downward.
Divination	Fortune-telling. The practice of trying to foretell the future by secret means.
Drupe	A fruit with a skin-covered fleshy outerpart which surrounds a hard, stone-like part which contains the seed . . . cherry, peach, plum (see poison ivy illustration).

Entire	Used when referring to leaf margin which is linear, not toothed or divided.

Follicle	A dry, many-seeded capsule or pod which opens along one side to release the seeds, like the milkweed pod.

Gall	A tumor on plant tissues caused by some exterior stimulation as a virus, fungus, insects (egg-laying), or bacteria.

Habit	The characteristic way a plant grows, such as twining, upright, reclining, etc.
Halberd	Shaped like an arrowhead but with the basal lobes spreading outward.

Inflorescence	The flowering part of a plant. The arrangement of several flowers on a flowering shoot. Almost always used for a flower cluster.
Infusion	A tea which results when plant matter is steeped in hot water.
Involucre	Any leaf-like structure which protects the reproductive structure of a plant, like the ring of small leaves at the base of a flower (see chicory illustration).

Kettle hole	A depression in the earth left after the melting of a buried block of ice left by the receding glacier.
Lanceolate	Lance-shaped. Longer than wide with widest part at the base and narrowing to apex.
Linear	Narrow, long, and with sides parallel or very near so.
Lobed (leaf)	Divided half-way to the midrib or less.
Logwood	The wood of a tropical tree *(Haematoxylon campechianum)* which yields a dye which was once used in dyeing fabrics.
Mericarp	A one-seeded portion of a fruit that splits up at maturity (see Queen Anne's lace illustration).
Mordant	A substance used to treat a material so that the color will remain fixed when dye is applied.
Native	Belonging to a locality or country by production, birth or growth. Not coming from a foreign area.
Naturalized	Refers to a plant which has come from a foreign area and has adapted to a new environment.
Node	Place where leaves or branchlets are attached to a stem.
Ocrea	A tubelike covering around the stems of some plants (see Lady's thumb illustration).
Opposite (leaves)	Two leaves or branchlets at the same node situated across the stem from one another.
Ovate (leaf)	Egg-shaped in outline and attached at the wide end.
Panicle	A branched raceme with each branch bearing a raceme (see mugwort and poison ivy illustrations).
Pappus	A ring or tuft of fine hairs which acts as a parachute for wind dispersal of seeds (see dandelion illustration).
Pedicel	Stalk of a single flower of an inflorescence.
Peduncle	Stalk of an inflorescence (flower cluster) or of a solitary flower which is not part of a cluster. Stalks of flowers in clusters are pedicels.

Perennial	A plant which lives for many growing seasons.
Persistent	Remaining attached after the growing season (see curly dock illustration).
Petiole	Stalk of a leaf.
Phyllary	A special name sometimes used for a bract of the involucre in composite plants (see burdock, daisy, dandelion illustrations).
Pistil	Seed producing organ of a flower.
Pistillate	Female flowered; one with seed-bearing organs (pistils) only, no pollen producing organs (stamens). (See sheep sorrel, amaranth, and yarrow illustrations.)
Poultice	A mass of hot, moist, soft material applied to a sore or inflamed part of the body.
Procumbent	Trailing, lying flat on the ground but not rooting.
Prostrate	Lying flat on the ground.
Pubescent	Covered with soft, short hairs.

Raceme	A single central stem which has single flowers, on their own stems, growing upward at intervals along it (see burdock and poke illustrations).
Ray	Strap-shaped flower in the outer part of a composite flower-head such as in the dandelion, chicory, or daisy; also, a branch of an umbel.
Recurved	Curved outward, backward, or downward.
Rhizome	An underground stem.
Root crown	The part of a root just below the surface of the ground where stem and root join.
Rootstock	Underground stem; rhizome.
Rosette	A dense, basal cluster of leaves arranged in a flat, whorled, or circular fashion as in chicory and mullein during their first years.

Scape	A leafless, or nearly leafless, stem rising from the ground (or center of a rosette) and bearing a flower or flower cluster, as in dandelion.

Schizocarp	A fruit that splits into mericarps at maturity (see Queen Anne's lace illustration).
Sessile	Without stem or petiole.
Sheathed	Surrounded by a long, more or less tubular structure (see ocrea).
Silicle	A short, broad pod of plants of the mustard family, with two parts (valves) that fall away from a thin central membrane which bears the seeds (see shepherd's purse illustration).
Simple (leaves)	Those which are not divided into completely different parts. Those in which the blade is all in one piece.
Spike	An inflorescence like a raceme, but the flowers of which are sessile (have no pedicels).
Staminate	Male-flowered. A plant with pollen-producing organs (stamens) only (see yarrow and sheep sorrel).
Stipule	Small papery leaf-like parts at the base of some petioles.
Succulent	Fleshy, soft, full of juice or water.
Tonic	Something which strengthens and invigorates the organism.
Toothed	Having a conspicuously sharply notched or indented margin.
Umbel	An umbrella-like flower cluster as in Queen Anne's lace.
Utricle	A small, thin-walled, one-seeded fruit (see amaranth and lambsquarters illustrations).
Valve	One of the parts into which a seedpod splits to discharge its seeds (see curly dock illustration).
Whorled	Three or more leaves, or other structures (such as flowers), arranged in a circle around a stem at the same node.

APPENDIX

COMMON NAMES

As we have seen, common names often suggest the uses to which plants have been put. Mats have been woven from cattails and one of the common names is mat-rush, for example. In Latin *personata* means "one who is masked." It was given to burdock as a common name because the large leaves of the plant are said to have been used as masks by actors in ancient Greece. Seeds of chickweed and plantain have been collected as food for birds and the plants have been called "birdseed." Because the seeds were often fed to small songbirds belonging to a group known as passerines, chickweed has also been named "passerina."

We have also seen that the list of common names for any plant may indicate several uses for it. Fine hairs painstakingly rubbed from mullein's velvety leaves were once twisted into wicks for candles and the name "candlewick" has become one of those by which the plant is known. There was a time when it was the practice to soak mullein's tall flower stalks in tallow and use them to light nighttime events. The name "torches" came from that use and the names "hag taper" and "witch taper" stem from the idea that the torches were used to light secret night ceremonies of witches.

That several names may describe the same use for a particular plant is illustrated by the names "soapwort," "latherwort," "scourwort," "soaproot," and "lady's washbowl" for bouncing Bet. Were the "l" in "lady's washbowl" capitalized, the name might be said to have originated in some real or fancied relationship with the Virgin Mary. As it is, the uncapitalized name tells us it comes from the plant's use by women in general.

Because the names have come from so many different sources over such a long period of time, reasons for them are not always so easily determined. Sometimes the words used are no longer a part of everyday speech and their meanings are almost forgotten. Felon herb, as a name for mugwort, is one such. Rarely do we run across the word "felon" to describe the painful pus-producing swellings that sometimes appear at the ends of fingers and toes. Once we have sought out its meaning, though, the name felon herb lets us know that the plant was once considered useful for treating such ailments. Poke is another puzzler. It has nothing to do with punching, and nothing to do with paper bags (called "pokes" in some parts of the country). As a plant name it is one of those words, like *personata*, which has worked its way into English from another language. It springs from *pocan*, as found in the name pocan bush, and *pocan* is derived from the American Indian word *puccoon* which means "a plant used for staining and dyeing."

While some people have considered a plant useful for a given purpose, others might have felt it was really useless or inferior for that purpose. In such cases words like "crow," "toad," and "dog" were often made a part of the common name. Thus "crow soap," for bouncing Bet, may have been given because someone saw a crow taking a bath in a puddle bordered by the plant, but it is more likely that the person who applied the name had tried to use the plant as soap and, finding it less than desired, tagged it with the appellation "crow."

There have been many common names listed for the plants included in the book. Not all of them describe a plant's use or uselessness. Names like bitter dock, silkweed, stinkweed, blackberry, and snapdragon tell how certain plants taste, feel, smell, look, or behave. Field ox-eye daisy, Mayweed, and carelessweed give some idea where, when, and how the plants grow. Sometimes the same name has been used to refer to several plants. At other times a number of different names have been used in referring to a single plant. By having them all listed alphabetically, as they are here along with their botanical names, confusions as to what plant is meant may be quickly cleared up. Of more importance, perhaps, is the fact that the reader who wants to make comparisons for himself, to speculate about reasons, meanings, and sources for the names, is not faced with the frustrating problem of having to shuffle endlessly back and forth through the pages to find the different names. Plants not yet listed for the islands are indicated by *.

NOTE:

For a variety of reasons, even botanists do not always use botanical names for the plants they write or talk about. If a botanist is talking to a group of non-botanists, for example, he may choose to use common names. As might be expected, though, the profusion of common names and the confusions they sometimes seem to generate have stimulated more than one effort, in this country and abroad, to standardize even the common names. Needless to say, the effectiveness of these efforts has been somewhat limited, but many of the plants *have* been assigned standardized common names and some attempts *are* made to use them.

In some ways these standardized names take the fun out of common names and may even obscure some rather interesting meanings. Look at the standardized common name for *Polygonum persicaria,* for example. It is "ladysthumb." Gone from it is the capital "L" and consequently any meaning it held for those who might recognize it as an indication that the plant and its history were related, in some way, to the Virgin Mary. And what sort of sense is there in including the "s" without the apostrophe?

Such questions raised by some of the names form a study in themselves. It is worth knowing, though, that an effort at standardization is being made, that there are some good reasons for it, and that it is meeting with varying degrees of success. The names, as they have been standardized for the plants in this book, are listed by themselves following the more inclusive listing.

COMMON NAMES

ailanthus .... *Ailanthus altissima*

amaranth .... *Amaranthus retroflexus*

amours .... *Malva neglecta*

antelope horn .... *Asclepias syriaca*

asparagus .... *Asparagus officinalis*

barberry .... *Berberis vulgaris*

bardana .... *Arctium minus*

beggar's buttons .... *Arctium minus*

bird seed .... *Plantago major*
Stellaria media

bird's nest .... *Daucus carota*

bitter buttons .... *Tanacetum vulgare*

bitter dock .... *Rumex crispus*

black bindweed ... *Polygonum convolvulus*

blackberry .... *Rubus spp.*

black-eyed susan .... *Rudbeckia hirta*

blackseed plantain ...... *Plantago rugelii*

blessed vegetable ..... *Portulaca oleracea*

blowball .... *Taraxacum officinale*

blue daisy .... *Cichorium intybus*

blue dandelion .... *Cichorium intybus*

blue sailors .... *Cichorium intybus*

boortree .... *Sambucus canadensis*

bouncing Bet .... *Saponaria officinalis*

brambles .... *Rubus spp.*

broad-leaved plantain .... *Plantago major*

buckhorn plantain ... *Plantago lanceolata*

bumpipe .... *Taraxacum officinale*

burdock .... *Arctium minus*

butter and eggs .... *Linaria vulgaris*

butter daisy .... *Ranunculus acris*

buttercup .... *Ranunculus acris*

Canada fleabane ..... *Erigeron canadensis*

candlewick .... *Verbascum thapsus*

careless weed .... *Amaranthus retroflexus*

carpenter's weed ..... *Achillea millefolium*

casewort .... *Capsella bursa-pastoris*

catnip .... *Nepeta cataria*

cat-o-nine-tails .... *Typha latifolia*

cattail .... *Typha latifolia*

cedar .... *Juniperus virginiana*

cheeses .... *Malva neglecta*

chickweed .... *Stellaria media*

chicory .... *Cichorium intybus*

chimney sweeps .... *Typha latifolia*

clappedepouch ... *Capsella bursa-pastoris*

clotbur .... *Arctium minus*

coast blite .... *Chenopodium rubrum*

coffeeweed .... *Cichorium intybus*
Rumex crispus

coltsfoot .... *Tussilago farfara*

common blue violet ... *Viola papilionacea*

common burdock .... *Arctium minus*

common cattail .... *Typha latifolia*

common chickweed ...... *Stellaria media*

common lambsquarters
Chenopodium album

common mallow .... *Malva neglecta*

common milkweed ..... *Asclepias syriaca*

common mullein ..... *Verbascum thapsus*

common purslane ..... *Portulaca oleracea*

common yarrow ..... *Achillea millefolium*

common yellow wood sorrel
Oxalis stricta

cow itch .... *Rhus radicans*

cow's eyes *Chrysanthemum leucanthemum*

cow's lungwort ...... *Verbascum thapsus*

crow soap .... *Saponaria officinalis*

cuckoo meat .... *Rumex acetosella*

curly dock .... *Rumex crispus*

cyrillo .... *Stellaria media*

daisy ..... *Chrysanthemum leucanthemum*

daisy fleabane .... *Erigeron annuus*

dandelion .... *Taraxacum officinale*

deadmen's daisy .....*Achillea millefolium*

Devil's milkpail.... *Taraxacum officinale*

Devil's nettle ....*Achillea millefolium*

Devil's plague .... *Daucus carota*

Devil's plaything ....*Achillea millefolium*

Devil's trumpet ...... *Datura stramonium*

dittander .... *Lepidium latifolium*

dodder ....*Cuscuta gronovii*

dog daisy.............. *Anthemis cotula*

doll cheeses.............. *Malva neglecta*

duckweed .... *Portulaca oleracea*

dyer's weed ....*Phytolacca americana*

elderberry .... *Sambucus canadensis*

farmer's curse
Chrysanthemum leucanthemum

felon herb .... *Artemisia vulgaris*

fiddle.................... *Daucus carota*

field ox-eye daisy
Chrysanthemum leucanthemum

fire-weed .... *Datura stramonium*
Plantago major

flannel leaf .... *Verbascum thapsus*

flaxweed.................*Linaria vulgaris*

flewort .... *Stellaria media*

flower of love ... *Amaranthus retroflexus*

frost blite........... *Chenopodium album*

gallwort ....*Linaria vulgaris*

garget ....*Phytolacca americana*

gentlemen's sorrel ..... *Rumex acetosella*

goldenrod .... *Solidago spp.*

goosefoot........... *Chenopodium album*

greytoad.............. *Artemisia vulgaris*

gunbright............. *Equisetum arvense*

hag taper .... *Verbascum thapsus*

healing blade .... *Plantago major*

heart's ease .... *Polygonum persicaria*

horse daisy.............. *Anthemis cotula*

horsetail.............. *Equisetum arvense*

Jacob's rod.......... *Verbascum thapsus*

Japanese knotweed
Polygonum cuspidatum

jealous woman .... *Arctium minus*

jewelweed ....*Impatiens spp.*

jimsonweed.......... *Datura stramonium*

knotweed.......... *Polygonum persicaria*

laceflower .... *Daucus carota*

ladies' sorrel............... *Oxalis stricta*

Lady's thumb ..... *Polygonum persicaria*

lady's washbowl .... *Saponaria officinalis*

lambsquarters ...... *Chenopodium album*

latherwort .... *Saponaria officinalis*

lesser trefoil .... *Trifolium dubium*

little vinegar-plant ..... *Rumex acetosella*

love me .. *Chrysanthemum leucanthemum*

lover's pride .... *Polygonum persicaria*

madapple............ *Datura stramonium*

malice .... *Malva neglecta*

markweed .... *Rhus radicans*

mat-rush ....*Typha latifolia*

Mayweed .... *Anthemis cotula*

*medick ....*Medicago arabica*

meld .... *Chenopodium album*

mercury .... *Rhus radicans*

milfoil...............*Achillea millefolium*

milkweed.............. *Asclepias syriaca*

mother's heart ... *Capsella bursa-pastoris*

mugwort .... *Artemisia vulgaris*

mullein .... *Verbascum thapsus*

nettle...................... *Urtica dioica*

oak .... *Quercus spp.*

orange day lily .... *Hemerocallis fulva*

ox-eye daisy
　　Chrysanthemum leucanthemum

palsywort .... *Stellaria media*

passerina .... *Stellaria media*

personata .... *Arctium minus*

pickle grass .... *Oxalis stricta*

pick-purse .... *Capsella bursa-pastoris*

pigeon berry .... *Phytolacca americana*

pigsty daisy .... *Anthemis cotula*

pigweed .... *Amaranthus retroflexus*
　　　　　　Chenopodium album
　　　　　　Portulaca oleracea

pike plant .... *Rumex crispus*

pissenlit .... *Taraxacum officinale*

plantain .... *Plantago major*

pocan bush .... *Phytolacca americana*

poison daisy .... *Anthemis cotula*

*poison hemlock ...... *Conium maculatum*

poison ivy .... *Rhus radicans*

poison oak .... *Rhus radicans*

poke .... *Phytolacca americana*

pokeweed .... *Phytolacca americana*

porcelain .... *Portulaca oleracea*

portulaca .... *Portulaca oleracea*

poverty weed
　　Chrysanthemum leucanthemum

prostrate knotweed . *Polygonum aviculare*

purple clover .... *Trifolium pratense*

purple-stemmed plantain *Plantago rugelii*

purslane .... *Portulaca oleracea*

pusley .... *Portulaca oleracea*

Queen Anne's lace .... *Daucus carota*
　　　　　　Trachymene caerulea
　　　　　　(cultivated)

rabbits .... *Linaria vulgaris*

ragged sailors .... *Cichorium intybus*

ragweed .... *Ambrosia artemisiifolia*

red knees .... *Polygonum persicaria*

red shanks .... *Polygonum persicaria*

red sorrel .... *Rumex acetosella*

red-ink berry ...... *Phytolacca americana*

redroot pigweed . *Amaranthus retroflexus*

reed mace .... *Typha latifolia*

rubber tree .... *Asclepias syriaca*

sailor's tobacco .... *Artemisia vulgaris*

St. James' weed . *Capsella bursa-pastoris*

St. John's plant .... *Artemisia vulgaris*

sambucus .... *Sambucus canadensis*

satin flower .... *Stellaria media*

scarlet pimpernel ...... *Anagallis arvensis*

schoolboy clock ... *Taraxacum officinale*

scouring rush .... *Equisetum arvense*

scourwort .... *Equisetum arvense*
　　　　　　Saponaria officinalis

seaside lambsquarters .... *Atriplex patula*

sheep poison .... *Oxalis stricta*

sheep sorrel .... *Rumex acetosella*

shepherd's purse . *Capsella bursa-pastoris*

shirt-button plant .... *Malva neglecta*

silkweed .... *Asclepias syriaca*

snakeweed .... *Plantago major*

snapdragon .... *Linaria vulgaris*

soaproot .... *Saponaria officinalis*

soapwort .... *Saponaria officinalis*

soldier's woundwort .. *Achillea millefolium*

sour dock .... *Rumex crispus*

sour grass .... *Oxalis europaea*
　　　　　　Oxalis stricta
　　　　　　Rumex acetosella

staghorn sumac .... *Rhus typhina*

stinking daisy .... *Anthemis cotula*

stinkweed .... *Datura stramonium*

sumac .... *Rhus typhina*

swallow-wort .... *Asclepias syriaca*

sweet clover .... *Melilotus alba*
Melilotus officinalis

sweet pepper-bush ...... *Clethra alnifolia*

*sweetfern ....*Comptonia peregrina*

swine snout........ *Taraxacum officinale*

tansy ....*Tanacetum vulgare*

thornapple .... *Datura stramonium*

thousand seal........*Achillea millefolium*

three-leaved ivy........... *Rhus radicans*

toad sorrel ....*Oxalis stricta*
Rumex acetosella

toadflax ....*Linaria vulgaris*

tongue grass............. *Stellaria media*

torches .... *Verbascum thapsus*

toyweed .... *Capsella bursa-pastoris*

tree of heaven ....*Ailanthus altissima*

tumble mustard.. *Sisymbrium altissimum*

tumbleweed ..... *Amaranthus retroflexus*

two-heads-entangled .. *Viola papilionacea*

violet................. *Viola papilionacea*

waiter-by-the-way..... *Cichorium intybus*

*water hemlock.......... *Cicuta maculata*

water torch...............*Typha latifolia*

waybroad .... *Plantago major*

white clover .... *Trifolium repens*

whiteman's foot .... *Plantago major*

wild beet .... *Amaranthus retroflexus*

wild spinach .... *Chenopodium album*

willow....................... *Salix spp.*

winterweed .... *Stellaria media*

wishes .... *Taraxacum officinale*

witch taper .... *Verbascum thapsus*

*wolf's milk .... *Euphorbia esula*

wood sorrel .... *Oxalis europaea*
Oxalis stricta

wormseed .... *Chenopodium album*

wormwood .... *Artemisia vulgaris*

yarrow ....*Achillea millefolium*

yellow dock .... *Rumex crispus*

yellow toadflax ....*Linaria vulgaris*

yellow wood sorrel ..... *Oxalis europaea*
Oxalis stricta

STANDARDIZED COMMON NAMES

Achillea millefolium L. . . . . common yarrow

Amaranthus retroflexus L. . . . . redroot pigweed

Arctium minus Bernh. . . . . common burdock

Artemisia vulgaris L. . . . . mugwort

Asclepias syriaca L. . . . . common milkweed

Capsella bursa-pastoris (L.) Medic. . . . . shepherdspurse

Chenopodium album L. . . . . common lambsquarters

Chrysanthemum leucanthemum L. . . . . oxeye daisy

Cichorium intybus L. . . . . chicory

Datura stramonium L. . . . . jimsonweed

Daucus carota L. . . . . wild carrot

Linaria vulgaris Mill. . . . . yellow toadflax

Malva neglecta Wallr. . . . . common mallow

Oxalis stricta L. common yellow woodsorrel

Phytolacca americana L. common pokeweed

Plantago major L. . . . . broadleaf plantain

Polygonum persicaria L. . . . . ladysthumb

Portulaca oleracea L. . . . . common purslane

Rhus radicans L. . . . . poison ivy

Rumex acetosella L. . . . . red sorrel

Rumex crispus L. . . . . curly dock

Stellaria media (L.) Vill. . . . . chickweed

Taraxacum officinale Weber . . . . common dandelion

Typha latifolia L. . . . . common cattail

Verbascum thapsus L. . . . . common mullein

SELECTED REFERENCES

If you wish to learn more about the history, folklore, and uses of the plants you find on the islands and elsewhere, the following selected references will help. Should you wish to know even more, most of the references contain their own lists which will make it possible to look further.

1) Agricultural Research Service of the United States Department of Agriculture. *Common Weeds of the United States.* Dover Publications, Inc., 1971.

2) Bailey, L. H. *How Plants Get Their Names.* Dover Publications, Inc., 1963.

3) Cocannouer, Joseph A. *Weeds: Guardians of the Soil.* The Devin-Adair Company, 1976.

4) Cole, John N. *Amaranth: From the Past, For the Future.* Rodale Press, Inc., 1979.

5) Coon, Nelson. *The Dictionary of Useful Plants.* Rodale Press/Book Division, 1977.

6) Coon, Nelson. *Using Wild and Wayside Plants.* Dover Publications, Inc., 1980.

7) Crockett, Laurence J. *Wildly Successful Plants.* Collier Books, 1977.

8) Fernald, Merritt Lyndon and Kinsey, Alfred Charles. *Edible Wild Plants of Eastern North America.* Revised by Reed C. Rollins. Harper and Row, Publishers, 1958.

9) Gerard, John. *The Herbal, or General History of Plants.* Dover Publications, Inc., 1975.

10) Gibbons, Euell. *Stalking the Blue-eyed Scallop. Stalking the Healthful Herbs. Stalking the Wild Asparagus.* David McKay Company, Inc., 1970.

11) Grieve, Mrs. M. *A Modern Herbal* (two volumes). Dover Publications, Inc., 1971.

12) Hatfield, Audrey Wynne. *How to Enjoy Your Weeds.* Collier Books, 1974.

13) Haughton, Claire Shaver. *Green Immigrants: The Plants that Transformed America.* Harcourt Brace Jovanovich, Inc./Harvest Book, 1978.

14) Healey, B. J. *A Gardener's Guide to Plant Names.* Charles Scribner's Sons, 1972.

15) Hedrick, U. P., editor. *Sturtevant's Edible Plants of the World.* Dover Publications, Inc., 1972.

16) Hussey, Jane Strickland. "Some Useful Plants of Early New England." Reprinted from *Economic Botany,* Vol. 28, No. 3, July-September, 1974, pp. 311-337.

17) Kingsbury, John M. *Deadly Harvest: A Guide to Common Poisonous Plants.* Holt, Rinehart and Winston, 1972.

18) Krochmal, Arnold and Connie. *A Guide to the Medicinal Plants of the United States.* Quadrangle/The New York Times Book Company, 1975.

19) Levering, Dale, PhD. *An Illustrated Flora of the Boston Harbor Islands.* Northeastern University Press, 1978.

20) Lovelock, Yann. *The Vegetable Book.* George Allen and Unwin, Ltd. For information, write: St. Martin's Press, Inc., 175 Fifth Avenue, N.Y., N.Y. 10010.

21) Lust, John. *The Herb Book.* Bantam Books, 1978.

22) Martin, Alexander C. *Weeds* (A Golden Guide). Webster Publishing Company, Inc., 1972.

23) Millspaugh, Charles F. *American Medicinal Plants: An Illustrated and Descriptive Guide to Plants Indigenous to and Naturalized in the United States Which are Used in Medicine.* Dover Publications, Inc., 1974.

24) Muenscher, Walter Conrad. *Poisonous Plants of the United States.* Collier Books, 1975.

25) Newcomb, Lawrence. *Newcomb's Wildflower Guide*. Little, Brown and Company, 1977.

26) Page, Nancy M. and Weaver, Richard E., Jr. *Wild Plants in the City*. Quadrangle/The New York Times Book Company, 1975.

27) Peterson, Lee. *A Field Guide to Edible Wild Plants of Eastern and Central North America*. Houghton Mifflin Co., 1978.

28) Peterson, Roger Tory and McKenny, Margaret. *A Field Guide to Wildflowers of Northeastern and Northcentral North America*. Houghton Mifflin Co, 1968.

29) Petry, Loren C. *A Beachcomber's Botany*. The Chatham Conservation Foundation, Inc., 1968.

30) Saunders, Charles Francis. *Edible and Useful Wild Plants of The United States and Canada*. Dover Publications, Inc., 1976.

31) Sherwood, Martha. *Collecting Roots and Herbs for Fun and Profit*. Greatlakes Living Press, 1978.

32) Shosteck, Robert. *Flowers and Plants: An International Lexicon with Biographical Notes*. Quadrangle/The New York Times Book Company, 1974.

33) Silverman, Maida. *A City Herbal: A Guide to the Lore, Legend, and Usefulness of 34 Plants that Grow Wild in the City*. Alfred A. Knopf, 1977.

34) Spencer, Edwin Rollin. *All About Weeds*. Dover Publications, Inc., 1974.

35) Wheelwright, Edith Grey. *Medicinal Plants and their History*. Dover Publications, Inc., 1974.

36) Wilder, Walter Beebe. *Bounty of the Wayside*. Doubleday, Doran and Co., Inc., 1943.

If your interests run to trees and shrubs the following guides will be helpful.

37) Symonds, George W. D. *The Shrub Identification Book*. William Morrow and Company, 1963.

38) Symonds, George W. D. *The Tree Identification Book*. William Morrow and Company, 1963.

For more information about the islands:

39) Kales, Emily and David. *All About the Boston Harbor Islands*. Herman Publishing Co. Inc., 1980.

40) Metropolitan Area Planning Council. *Boston Harbor Islands Comprehensive Plan*. Massachusetts Department of Natural Resources, 1972.

41) Mikal, Alan. *Exploring Boston Harbor*. The Christopher Publishing House, 1975.

42) Snow, Edward Rowe. *The Islands of Boston Harbor*. Dodd, Mead and Co., 1971.

About poisonous plants.

43) See 17 and 24.

44) Howard, Richard A.; DeWolf, Gordon, Jr.; and Pride, George H. "Poisonous Plants." Reprint from *Arnoldia*, Vol. 34, No. 2, Mar./April 1974.

INDEX

spring tonic – 32
spurge – 31
stains, to remove – 34
starch – 28
Stellaria media – see chickweed
sterility – 41
sties – 43
stomach disorders – 29, 32, 43
strewing herbs – 24
string – 41
Sturtevant, Edward Lewis – 99
sugar – 41
sumac – 24
sunstroke – 30
sweet clover – 24
sweet pepper-bush – 24
sweetfern – 30
swellings – 43, 44
syrup – 28

T

Tanacetum vulgare – 23, 24, 26
tansy – 23, 24, 26
Taraxacum officinale – see dandelion
tarts – 38, 81
tea – 29, 32, 34, 35, 39, 40, 44, 63, 77
teeth – 28
thirst, to quench – 34, 42
Thompson's Island – 17, 47, 53, 55, 57, 59,
    63, 67, 71, 75, 77, 79, 81, 83, 85, 87, 89,
    91, 93, 95, 97, *104*-105
Thoreau – 33
thread – 41
tobacco substitute – 32, 40
toothache – 28, 40, 43
torches – 67, 113
toys – 24-25, 37, 39, 42, 44
Trachymene caerulea – 83
tree-of-Heaven – 26
Trifolium dubium – see lesser trefoil
Trifolium pratense – see purple clover
Trifolium repens – see white clover
tumor – 37
Typha spp. – see cattail
typhus – 41

U

ulcers – 37
Urtica spp. – see nettle

V

vegetables (pot herbs, etc.) – 27, 29, 32, 33,
    35, 38, 39, 44
Verbascum thapsus – see mullein
vermin – 23
vests, to stuff – 28
violet – 24-25
Viola papilionacea – 24-25
Virgin Mary – 40, 113, 114

W

"war" among plants – 65
warts – 41
wasps – 23
water hemlock – 38
weather – 34-35, 53
webbing – 28
weed repellent – 36
whistle – 25
wicks – 33
wild beast, to protect from – 30
wild mustard – 103
willow – 25
wine – 15, 24, 32
witches – 36
wolf's milk – 31
wood sorrel – see sorrel
woodenware, to clean – 24
woolen goods, to protect – 24
wounds – 33

Y

yarrow – 15, 23, 30, 39, 42, 53, 75, *86,* 87,
    101, 102, 103, 104